Kudos Honor New Book
Autobiography of god

The sometimes bewildering array of New Age affirmations and self development essays relating to spiritual growth has often left me with a feeling that the many authors are just copying one another's writings. Not so with Dr Herbert L Beierle's newest work, the *Autobiography of god*. The book providing refreshing insights, uplifts the inner spirit and lets our mind synchronize with the tides of time and truth. I have read Dr Beierle's book with much interest and delight.

To be and to do as Spirit is and does might be a global paraphrase of this excellent treatise. Certainly, without exception, Dr Beierle presents a refreshing look at the reality of our beingness and its relationship to the whole. God, as man, in man and man as god is, as presented in the *Autobiography of god* reveals anew one of the greatest secrets of life, realized and known only to a few enlightened souls down through the ages of history.

What an enchanting book! Read it; study it; meditate on its refreshing concepts of age old truths articulated exceptionally well, and you will say with me, "Well done, my good and faithful servant."

I, without reservation, highly recommend it to the many persons involved and associated with the twentieth and now twenty-first century religious thought and practice.

Al Lowe, PhD, AP, CAP Former Superintendent of Education
Miami, Florida

A Useful Road Map

As someone who loves to drive making a living and for fun, I know, before I get behind the wheel that my most important and useful tool will be a map!

As someone who is searching for spiritual awareness, I know that my most important and useful tool is an inner knowledge gained from hearing, living and reading.

THE AUTOBIOGRAPHY OF GOD by Herbert L Beierle is to understanding spiritual awareness as a map by THOMAS BROTHERS is to understanding the highways and streets I drive.

Michael L Stewart, Tow Truck Driver
Tacoma Washington

Autobiography of god

Herbert L Beierle

First Edition 1979

Campo California 91906-3213

Cover Photo Courtesy NASA

PRINTED IN THE UNITED STATES OF AMERICA

Also by Herbert L Beierle

The Art And Science Of Wholeness

Song Of The Spirit

Illumination, Handbook Of Ascended Masters

Autobiography Of god

The Relative

The Relative/Absolute

ABSOLUTE

Practitioners Manual

Ministers Manual

A Gift From Self To Self

I Am Number One

My Inner Journey

The Weathering

Quiet, Healing Zone!

Why I Can Say I Am God

How To Give A Healing Treatment

Practice Reality

Three Hour Meditation

The Law Of Cause And Effect

The Inexhaustible Laughter Of Heaven—BLISS

Many of these books are available in German, Italian, French and Russian.

ISBN 0-940480-38-7

UNI PRESS
1101 Far Valley Road, Campo California 91906-3213 USA

CONTENTS

Dedication

This book is dedicated to people everywhere who know, have known, or will know that sense of inner awareness of being god.

—The Author

1

LITTLE "g" GOD!

A reasonable question anyone might ask is how does the *Autobiography of god* come to be written?

To answer this question we come to the definition of "god" and what it means, and what is included in that definition.

God is all.

God is nothing.

I am god. I am you the reader.

I am god. I am not giving "g" on god a lower case through humility. I am beyond that. As the wind is not capitalized not the sea, or the sky, or the snow, or the sand, or the star—so ubiquitous are they and so all, and I god am all "their all" and the infinity beyond that; hence, lower case "g"!

God is in, through and as all that ever was, ever will be, ever was not, ever will not be and our cynosure: the focal point of our admiration and interest, our guide and center of our attention.

The redundancy of such a statement is so obvious and so curt that anyone reading it will feel insecure and unfulfilled.

So it behooves us to be more specific in drawing our conclusion.

To say that god is all means that as the creative cause of the universe that which creates anything *is itself that creation.*

That which creates anything dwells in that which it creates. Thus god is its creation of a *tree* as the *tree* representing all that the creator conceives of a *tree* as being.

So the *tree* is meant to be a vegetative growing entity with roots, bark and leaves. It is a woody perennial plant with its one main trunk from which it develops its branches, usually at some height from the ground; or anything resembling a *tree* in structure of form.

This seems simple enough.

However, *are* we able to accept the *tree* as

being all of god or even being part of god, or in any way to represent god?

To this we can only say a resounding **yes**, that is just what we must accept if we are to proceed with any premise about what god is and how to understand god in its allness.

At the outset it might be wise to recognize that each individual creation of god is designed to express an aspect of its allness, and while it does not at any one moment appear to express all of its allness, all of its allness dwells in each aspect of its allness. God can never be dissected or separated from itself at any time, even while appearing to be less than all of its nature or reality.

Within the *tree* is all of god.

Expressing is the nature of god as the *tree*.

Should the essence and form of the *tree*, its atomic structure and nature, at any instant be thought to be different than a *tree*—by its creator—the matter would return to its undifferentiated chaotic nothingness and instantly form into that which was conceived different from its former appearance as a *tree*.

Does this change the reality of god in the *tree* or in the new form it assumes: not one little bit. All that god is was present before and is now present in its new form.

The variety of expression of god in, through, and as all that it conceives itself as being gives diversity to the nature of the appearance while never changing the nature of the creator.

So, from this point of view, we shall be looking

at god and its various appearances and why, regardless of appearance, that outpictured issue, though not reflecting our conception of god, is indeed god and all of god. Whatever is expressed is what god as that expression desires to express of its divine self at that particular point in time and space in the game of life.

Here we shall find that animal, mineral, vegetable as well as the "nothingness" and chaos or undifferentiated matter, are all expressions of the infinite creative cause shining forth the apparently solid illusion of dynamic variety and yet sameness.

We shall read about creation in every aspect of its creativeness. We shall learn about morality and what role it has to play in the remarkable program of things. We shall open our eyes to a new view of just what life is and how it is utilized in objects both animate and inanimate, seen and unseen.

Once we have walked through my charming *Autobiography of god*, the mystery will yet remain for few could understand the intricacies sufficiently unraveling the purpose for which all has been designed; however, we will be one step nearer to nonjudgmentally and unconditionally enjoying this experience through which we are living.

Now, with the insights from what we read here, we can lovingly release the old fetishes which we have believed in because we did not understand them and were bound in their superstitious and magical power, to a fresh freedom through an inner wisdom into the nature and being of the creative cause of all, god.

Happy venturing!

2

WHAT DO MEN SAY I AM

I am the infinite, I am the ultimate, I am the all.

I am without beginning and without end, for there is neither time nor place in which a beginning or end could exist.

Within the consciousness of all creation, which I am, I plant the awareness of my essence and my allness—for I am within all of my creation with the allness which I am and always will be.

Though I might express myself as a finite appearance or illusion, what is seen is only a glimpse of the stability and reality which is my nature. No matter who might wish to know me they will only know me by knowing themselves. For I am they who would know me and I am that which they wish to know. I am very knowable and I am always known. Only those who pretend at knowing reality say that it cannot be known. All who would know me and know who and what I am already know it all and enjoy it and that which I am—the fullest expression of the finest nature which each is and always will be.

Who You Think You Are Is Who You Think I Am!.

Everyman seeks out a reason for existence. Everybeing labels the world about him in the scope and dress of his own thoughts and his own philosophy of life—his own religion—that which primarily he would think about and believe in.

This philosophy has built-in limitations. It has the idea that it is a universal truth while generally it is a very localized "truth" consistent for the thinker alone. This need not be the condition, but it is to those who bind themselves in such tight patterns of awareness and belief that it does not allow for the imagination and dreams others have for themselves.

The wisest expression of myself, that is—one which encompasses the broadness of my reality—is the one which allows for everyone's imagination to play in the field of dreams. I am the ultimate, therefore I am the expression of the vast horizons of thoughts and dreams of all of creation—all of myself! I love it too.

So now as I let myself be myself through my expression or creation, all who give soaring reign to their thought world of grand imagination come closest to the potentiality and reality which I am.

One point here which is extremely vital for every thinker: Everything thought may or may not be true; everything dreamed may or may not be viable; everything imagined in consciousness may or may not be constructive for the pattern each would be seeking for themselves.

The purpose of my creation, for me, is to express myself.

The purpose of my creating anything is to have a joyfilled time in revealing the limitless potential of the possibilities which lay alive within every expression of me.

The purpose of my thinking myself into expression through and as the revelations, which shine forth who and what I am, is for me to gaily open the vistas of infinite probabilities as possibilities, as realities!

There is no other purpose for my existence, for the universe to exist, for the life (and apparent nonlife forms) for flowing forth into appearance and interacting one with another.

I am god and I am without any significant or real purpose for doing anything which I do.

Since I am the mind of those whom I create, those who and that which I create contain me, all of me, and are thus GOOD AND VERY GOOD and lovely in my sight.

I expect nothing more out of my creation than to be the vastness of my potentiality. It does not matter whether they APPEAR to be good or bad, they are always good in my sight, for they are me. It does not matter that they appear to be purely an illusion changeable and variable with every changing wind or thought flowing over the vast variety of possibilities to which the thought may be heir.

I am god.

I am good.

I am me.

All that is is me.

All that is is good.

All that is is whatever it is for no other reason than that it is what it is. I could never judge myself in my creation. I can only delightfully play the game of being me through all that exists to express me in varied ways.

Games I Play

All is a game, but a very definite game, with rules established by me in the guise of myself being the benefactor and the players in each game being played.

Looking at some of these games I see the magic of my being in the diverse costumes which I wear being me and being all.

I play games with myself and with you, and therefore you as I, know that what follows is not definitive, for to be in even any way nearly complete would require a volume unequaled in the imagination of humanity. So we shall play with just a few of the adventures that I create myself playing as my creation.

As an illustration we look at major world religions such as Christianity, Judaism, Buddhism, Hinduism and Islam. These only begin to include the variety of religions and merely point to the wonderment of humanity getting inside itself to know itself.

All major world religions have a similar basis. Even those religions which do not have an apparent anthropomorphic deity at the head of their teaching, should we look closer, we will find they have deified the Sun, the planets, plants and trees, volcanoes and mountains, animals and other creatures—investing in these things a humanistic melee. The confusion of this type of response seems to many to be inarticulate and unlettered, while actually what major religions have done with their deification of God and the messengers attributed to their God are equally as bizarre with its incongruities and "to others" unbelievable references.

No matter how unique and inexplicable is the history and the creative complexities of the deity for each and every religion or philosophy, one thing remains true for each: the deity is greater than the individual, it is more powerful than any other being, and strangely enough the deity is irascible, as though unconscionable of the devotion and dedication of its followers or adherents.

Seemingly the five religions of consequence followed by the majority of humanity are more logical, ethical and beneficent. Yet within each dwells an illogical, unethical and nonbeneficial quality—as it seemingly defies reason—in saying that something **which is the all** might ever **need** something from its creation. Smile! How strange. Also illogical is to think that the great creative cause **needs** its creation to express itself in any realistic way. The irrationality continues as these devotees believe that their God can one moment love its creation and another moment hate its creation and make a judgment about its creation when from the beginning the creator called its creation "good and very good" virtually in all religions.

I am whatever I am at all times. I cannot be coerced to be different from what my nature is—always being all which I am. Since I am "good" all of my creation is good at all times.

❑ Christianity

Each religion has a uniqueness about it which is defined by its interpreters. Each touches a lodestone within causing them to think that they have a very special awareness of the divine creative cause—and truly they do—and certainly so may every being go directly to the divine inherently within, the centrum of their focus for their everpresent reality. In the Bible God speaks in the third person; I always stand up for what and who I am.

It is no surprise there are many religions. The surprise might more readily be that there are not actually recognized 6.5 billion religions on the face of planet Earth, one for each citizen living here. And, of course, the infinite number of beings existing on this planet whom humanity reading this do not realize are present, and the infinite number of beings present on other planes in this vast universe—and the expression of myself in the unlimitable ways awaiting to be described to my creation, by myself, in my heart of hearts, each beholding **their** unique religion.

Christianity is defined in the *New Testament* as the philosophy of life professed by a person who believes Jesus the Christ came forth demonstrating that monotheistic God lives in the Christ spirit incarnate in all men. It claims the purpose of the philosophy of religion is to teach the way of life of a decent and respectable person. This includes, among other things, living a loving, kind and humble life.

Those who follow the teachings of this philosophy find that it claims there is one God and that God is omnipresent, omniscient and omnipotent. The Christian definition of God is of one who is the God of all creation, recognized or not, and he is a loving, fatherly and beneficent being having no equal.

These same qualities are consistent in all religions though they may define the Christian God as the first cause or some other term, the meaning is the same.

I laugh and sit back in smiling repose as I listen to one religion or even a segment of any religion within itself, belittle beliefs which propound that I am other than a loving presence and that for justice I will afflict anger or retribution upon my creation. A Law of cause and effect brings this into expression by the individual use of each of my creation. The illusion of love causes love, the illusion of hate causes hate, the illusion of life causes life, and the illusion of death causes the appearance of death. Any cause can be put into motion by the individual expression of myself itself for itself and as an illusion in the game being played—and also it can be changed at any moment should it choose to do so.

The divine man Jesus listened to the spirit of God in him and lived his life based upon this understanding. He recognized that the "Christ" represented something much greater than just the manself he was. Previous writings told of his coming and his life. He, however, insisted that what he did others could do also and greater things than he did everyone was capable of doing. His life is reported to have been a total dedication to his inner self.

The Christian ethic stands as a commendable basis for all creation since it does not in and of itself exclude any other of my creation from its utilization. Some adherents of this teaching and philosophy read into this religion a principle of exclusion. This is perfectly suitable and okay. Any game any wish to play is satisfactory for the great I am neither judges nor demands—it just IS.

❑ Judaism

Judaism is an effective religion throughout its history and is the foundation for two other major religions whose history sets firmly in the Jewish traditions and teachings, namely Christianity and Islam.

Coming out of the convictions and belief of the tribe of Judah, a group of Semitic peoples, the Hebrews trace their descendency and decency from Abraham, Isaac and Jacob for the Jewish religion. The faith in a monotheistic presence with traditions based on the laws and teaching of its scriptures and the *Talmud* and *Torah* with emphasis upon living a moral, traditional and ceremonious life. Ethical behavior is the true worship of God.

The *Old Testament* is the story of the religious development of a people, as is the holy book of any religious culture. It tells of the events which have led this group of people who are held together by specific traditions, desires, cultural mores and ethical behavior founded upon a philosophical background which is meaningful to them.

Though the conditions which were necessary for the studies and the concepts which conditioned the experiences of these people are vastly changed from that which they passed through centuries before, even thousands of years earlier, the religious leaders base current attitudes upon the old ways though it does not enhance the meliorism of the people and their lot is not thereby improved.

Strongly proposing a monotheistic God, basing the teaching on high ethical behavior, the desire to make or become better, to improve the lot of the people by ameliorating their life style left much to be desired and historically the "nation" was torn apart by other nations, only to compound their own inner stability and desire to be reunited as soon as possible. They say of me: *That thou art.*

I am always I am.

Always I speak from the center of each being representing the freedom to be myself in all I do regardless whether it may be interpreted as either positive or negative.

The religious philosophical greats who have so nobly given their stories through the ages expand and enlighten my voice through them. The books of the *Old Testament* reveal this well. Not one is more vital than another to the Judaic tradition. The *Song of Solomon*, *Proverbs*, *Psalms*, the story of *Job*, all reveal a person or a people searching within themselves for their divine center and in some ways finding it and in other ways having it elude them most critically. All of the time the search goes on the story of the religious and philosophical development of a people shines forth in every glorious manner revealing the diversity of the human being seeking its divinity.

I delight immeasurably in the expression of my unlimited self through all of my creation in whatever ways it might shine forth. I judge not and essentially allow total freedom to each expression so that it will be that flamboyant freespirited self which I am in all that it is.

The only limit placed upon my creation is the limitation it places on itself. It is absolutely free to be and do whatever it dreams or visualizes for itself. However it imagines itself is how I imagine it. This is why the seemingly epic struggles the Jews have experienced do not deter its adherents from holding on and reaching out for their ultimate fulfillment.

These remnants of so ancient a religion still taste the essence and the tang of their beloved

Talmud encompassing the writings which constitute the civil and religious law in both *Mishna* for the text and the *Gemara* with its commentary—the code by which life has its most significant meaning to a believer, a *Jew*.

❑ Islam

Islam. A generic people arise from time to time in various areas of the world seeking to develop a faith which fits most naturally the psychology, the physiology and the historic ethic of their personal life. Sometimes they succeed and on the wings of their faith soar into marvelous prominence in the world. The mystics of Islam are the sufis. The sufis fast from worldly thoughts at special times as Ramadan.

Sometimes the religious philosophy which is born of such a search lifts the people for only a short time helping them through great tribulations, but other times the milieu so gained serves as a cultural environment to better the people and then in a flash dies away having served its temporary purpose.

The Muslim religion based on the sacred book of *Islam* as written by Mohammed revealing the philosophy as given by Allah, the *Koran*, teaches a monotheistic religion. There are great similarities to the Hebraic *Old Testament* used commonly by the Christians and Jews.

Fundamental differences arise in the manner in which the teachings are carried out and the intensity of the services. All have a very overt conduct of worship which seemingly makes the esoteric lesson formerly available to the inner group only now less confidential, and indeed exoteric—knowable to the public.

Generically these religious philosophies are borne out of specific regions on Earth for the benefit of the clan or group seeking spiritual guidance. As the world became smaller through communication and travel, and as the various philosophies spread, people of every nationality and persuasion are enlightened by the sensitive and wise words of each faith making the brotherhood expansively grow. This was not only true of Islamic teachings but all others also.

Interestingly, every belief has indigenous within it some very powerful training seemingly not so powerfully present in another faith. While Christianity had education as its present goal through its development over the centuries, it was a closed education consistent with what its authorities allowed to be believed. The Muslims on the other hand were universal in their educational studies and encompassed every possible field of interest and each to the fullest depth conceivable at that time. Only in the adherence to its religious code of ethics was it unyielding. Christianity during the crusades and other moments of its history also became absolutely unyielding. In their unyielding quality legions have been slaughtered in the name of religion. And who is to say that religion, philosophy, belief and/or conviction are not all of the same ilk. And I, the great I am, judge not one jot or iota. All just is and without right or wrong, or good or bad. Allah, God, speaks in the Koran in the first person, as is my nature.

The *Koran* is a very powerful record of the manner in which Allah would have humanity live and express itself. It does not relate itself solely to its own ethnic group or nationalistic majority, but rather to all of mankind. In this it is a somewhat rare philosophy and kindly includes a great deal and allows for all races of men and all cultures to be enfolded in its embrace.

❑ Buddhism

Great leaders emerge from obscurity at various times throughout history without any seeming purpose or even a need. They come forth to spring into the consciousness of the multitude and spark an interest in selfrenewal and selfawareness beyond anything that had taken place for centuries, one way or the other, at that point.

The story of Lao Tse, Confucius, Jesus the Christ, Zoroaster, Mohammed, Buddha, Akhenaton, Socrates, and many notable others who turned the philosophical and religious world topsy-turvy, brought forth a new impulsion, a new breath of freshness to the staid stable religious convictions of its day. The Tao teaches: *To the mind that is still the world surrenders.*

His followers felt Siddhartha Gautama represented divine wisdom and virtue and named him the Buddha. His teaching was simplicity itself, as all great philosophies and religions are at their core, telling its adherents that right thinking (meditation) and deeds would enable each one who persisted in this direction to enable their soul to reach Nirvana, the divine state of release from misdirected desire.

His teaching was so simple he would hold before his followers simple objects for their meditation and consideration. He would ask each one to find within themselves their center of peace, of ultimate wisdom. He pointed out that everyone is wise as they thought him, and only as each one claimed this wisdom would they experience the wisdom they sought.

Appearing almost six hundred years before Christianity was born, Buddha came between other great philosophers who sought a practical way out of the clutches of reincarnation, being born again and again in an never ending cycle of rebirths.

Strangely his offering to those who would listen to his words was an existence of nothingness, a void, named Nirvana or better understood as bliss. Because he was such a startling living example of his belief, thousands upon thousands flocked to him to learn of his way.

Along with Hinduism which existed parallel to his time, he spoke as with the sages and gurus who all insisted that everyman is God. Without hesitation they and he taught: *I am God.* He taught one driving principle, many Gods as aspects of that monotheistic unity. This was not something unique or radical for these people or this time since being God was not the omni universal being as it was meant in the Christian-Islamic-Judaic tradition. It was, however, a step into the right direction. Though the Buddhistic and Hindu Gods were limited and specific, though numberless, as were the Greek and Roman Gods and Gods of the early Babylonians whose cultural melee was expressing about the same time as the teaching of the Buddha, what Buddha meant was that within everybeing is a divine presence which can be known and expressed and lived in a very real way.

His teaching reflected the laissez-faire attitude of letting people do as they pleased without official interference or direction. He was insistent upon the thesis: *Within every being is the divine, within everyone is bliss and their wholeness. Within each is the capacity to know itself and experience Nirvana now*. To this end his life was dedicated and directed.

Buddhism spread as the trade routes of its day expanded mostly to the east and to the southeast. In that way his effect was felt primarily in the Far East, the Middle East and Europe while other areas of the globe were untouched by his teaching. Only later when followers of Buddhism traveled the length and breadth of the Earth did Buddhism flower internationally where it met avid eager audiences.

All of these leaders of religions and philosophies were listening to a divine message from within. They taught that all may listen within themselves and hear the message of peace and beauty and love, if they tune their ear to their blissful center.

I express myself through many voices, through many visions, through many dreams, through many illusions—always me, the I am god in all.

❑ Hinduism

Most religions and philosophies are the result of combinations. As new religions sweep in the old are either swept out, swept under the rug, or joined with the new to form not only a new teaching, but a teaching somewhat like the new and the old. The ultimate is defined as: *Oh, thou, whom before all, worlds recoil.*

This happened to Judaism as it incorporated the tribal customs and pagan rituals thought foul at one time, but to incorporate the peoples who followed those beliefs, it was necessary to include their worship programs, with slight modifications. This was done in Mexico by the Catholics and Indian worship programs; with the American Indians and early Catholics and Christians; throughout the world; with the religious cultures surrounding the Mediterranean wherein all were busy in easy commercial congress one with the other.

Hinduism is a social religion with customs which are utilized in everyday life and thereby religious and family and business activities were all bound up in the same program—religious, philosophical, psychological and customs, all one—and all were viewed from the same pattern.

The religious and cultural program or way of life was primarily Brahmaistic in the early days with elements of Buddhism and Jainism, as well as other minor religious affectations in the Indian area, were out of one pattern.

The content of the Indian religion is the worship of Brahma, the supreme and eternal essence of the universe and chief member of the trinity including Vishnu and Siva, the creator of the universe.

Interestingly the caste system of Brahmanism came into the Buddhistic teachings, though they were not greatly emphasized. Because of this the full power of the Buddha's teachings were watered down and the full potential of the Hinduistic philosophy never reached its zenith, however it was massively practiced by the multitudes.

Hinduism taught one divine principle, and the many Gods as aspects of the principle. It teaches life in all its forms is an aspect of the divine—that which dwells within with—pure past, pure deeds and pure revelations or acts.

What Do Men Say I AM!

Men say that I am whatever they conceive me to be.

Men have the capacity to understand me as they understand themselves. Only as I look within and find myself will I be able to look at the creation of mine about me and know that it is myself being reflected there. It is only as I am one with that which I am can I understand what my reality truly is.

As is noted, every religion, every philosophy, every cultural ethic views itself solely upon what it conceives itself to be. If that system sees itself limited in any way, purely because it is searching for something within itself, then that is how it will "create" its world and populate its world with citizens limited as it is itself.

Until I am able to see myself unlimited, until men can see themselves, I AM, unlimited, free to be whatever they dream and yet not be limited by that dream they see themselves being, the world will be entirely too small. Their God will be entirely too small.

Once I am free in the soul of each of my creation to be what I eternally am, the realm of expression will explode and express so much more grandly than anyone ever could conceive of it being. The choice is mine.

It does not matter what men say I am, I am always that which I am, I am all. I am the absolute total ultimate reality of all. This sounds rather complete and fabulous and so it is. ∞

3

AS god I AM

This is my autobiography—I am god!

I am everything seen and unseen. I am that which exists and that which does not exist. I am the reality dwelling in thought and I am the illusion which never was nor ever will be, yet give every appearance of being reality to all which observe me as illusion.

It is through thought that a relative awareness of myself appears. It can ever be my reality. My reality is that which is me in my neverchanging nature. My reality is that which is true today, tomorrow and forevermore, regardless of the eons of relative illusions through which any creative consciousness, which I have created, observes me in expression.

I speak here to a relative audience of my mundane expression. From this point of view I share relative values. Be it known, all that I share is the illusory universe, for this is that which this creation knows.

In my absolute nature there is no time nor space, there is no illusion, there is no being or not being, all just is and as an IS is relationless and purposeless. So at the outset of my sharing here I may be quite clear that I am exploring the most infinitesimal aspect of my beingness, my elusive nature, which by its very nature is unreal and not everlasting. So, having this aside at this point in thinking, I am free of the absolute awareness, and play the game of the relative and have the ***time of my life****.*

I Am Infrangible

Since my expression in the mundane world is an appearance of whatever I choose at whatever moment I choose to choose it, I am infrangible—I cannot be separated or violated. Everything I do I do because it pleases me to do just that. I am unbreakable, unbendable in my *moral strength based upon solid principle.*

For each experience I choose to play, animal, mineral or vegetable—or whatever—I write up the game plan for that action and that expression.

I do not have a conditional morality about whatever it is that I choose to play.

Should I be a plant, I do not have the feeling that I should or should not be eaten, I should or should not be trampled upon by whatever should come my way—I am without presentiment or foreboding, for indeed I have within my awareness everything which will take place in my proposed life span, the program of my existence. All things that happen are neither good nor of an evil unfortunate nature.

Out of the infinite possibilities, I have chosen a variety of projections. I have not tied myself to any one series of possibilities, but I have opened myself to the probabilities based on how I carry out each action and what—at that moment—seems an exciting potentiality for me.

This immediately releases any presumption of destiny or fate. However, as I utilize the Law of cause and effect to bring about any effect in my experience, the seemingly inevitable or necessary succession of events would take place **UNLESS I** decided to place a new set of causes in motion for a new effect contrary and even totally ambiguous to what seemingly is my best advantage. Should I release any ambivalence toward my choice and stand firm for one conviction, that one alone then **could** manifest, depending upon my onepointedness.

So early in my thinking I consider the plant I choose to be. I thought of me being eaten or trampled upon and found that neither of these actions could be considered as unfortunate. Every and all actions and events in the life of the plant, or any creation, are bound to two distinct conditions relative to their existence and expression.

One condition is that of the Law of cause and effect, and the other condition is the realization of the unreality of the relative world drawing whatever it is that it desires to be and do, regardless of any causes or outward situations.

It seems I am bringing a curve ball here directing my thinking to a circumstance for which I am not prepared. If, indeed, I am responsible to the Law of cause and effect, how then, can I obviate that Law which is totally intractable and intransigent. The Law of cause and effect is unchangeable, stubborn, uncompromising and effective. By putting a new cause in motion the old cause ceases to be effective—but apparently only by the putting of a new cause in motion.

The second condition is effective when the total awareness of the illusory nature which existence expresses is seen through and all validity is taken from any thought which validates it. At this point that which seems to be real turns into an illusion and as a phantasm it loses all perception as something which has physical reality. Naturally, at that instant, it ceases apparent reality and its phantom apparition fades from view.

Smile, I can see the expression being given by some for these illusive remarks.

Why do I even talk about it when all is so unreal, all is only the reception of a mental image or representation—something existing in the mind of the thinker. As I understand this clearly I understand what expression on the relative universe is all about. All is an illusion, however an illusion of the mind.

Relative Illusion's Stage

It is in the mind in which all of the theatrics take place for the illusion in the relative world. The mind is the great staging ground for all of the activities, the prethought thinking and the afterthought thinking. The thinking itself is but an infinitesimal fraction of the total picture. Most time is spent by any thinker in fore or after thought.

To accomplish the fulfillment of any thought, of any illusion, the onepointed action of the thinker thinking such thoughts brings them into expression and fulfillment for the relative being.

Thought completes this expression for all of my creation.

The plant is thought of being a unit of my creation that does not think. This is an attitude which I create many other beings having about plants, minerals and animals. However all think! For ALL are me, and I think, therefore all think!

The plant can **create itself** in fertile ground, under the finest atmospheric conditions, in the most plush surroundings harmonious to its growth and maturation in its most joyous way. OR—the plant can **create itself** in infertile unrelenting ground in which it gains little hold and sustenance. The plant can create about it too much sun, too much rain, too much traffic, too much of everything not leading to its tranquil harmonious existence. Each environment is established by the thinking of the individual expression of myself doing what it chooses for the fun of expressing in just that manner.

Nothing happens by chance in the relative world. Everything has a cause behind it which has brought it into expression in just the manner which it is now using.

This harkens back to destiny or fate—wrong!

This harkens to the making of choices which I do constantly so long as I **enjoy** expressing in my relative world. I like who I am, what I am doing, how I am living, who are my friends, every single experience I have—I like it and I choose it.

Indeed:

NOTHING HAPPENS BY CHANCE IN THE RELATIVE WORLD.

Even when I seek to reach beyond the relative and slip into the mode of the infinite, the absolute, it is my choice. These choices are what make my existence a joy or a tragedy.

Getting back to my plant friend—I ask why any selfrespecting plant would ask for itself less than salubrious conditions under which to live. Surprise, I could ask the same thing of all of my creation, all expressing and being me!

Since there is no judgment, no condition, no possession, only the purest of joy and love in doing all which I do, then even what appears evil is truly meant for good.

Some have said:

Man meant it for evil,
god meant it for good!

What does this mean?

Simply, it means that in all the universe everything which exists is good and very good—where have I heard that before—and therefore everything is good and very good and cannot be otherwise. I, god, mean everything that is—being an expression of me, and being me—is good and very good because it is ME.

I could ask why the plant would want to live in soil conditions which are sour, dry, acid or in any way not harmonious for good functional growth—because it is a game, because it is amusing. Should a plant want to feel pain, it would. Should a plant want to be dry or hot, wet or cool, abundant or limited—anything at all—it may do just that and only itself is at cost.

Whatever thoughts go through the mind and thinking system of any creation of mine, this is what I have it experience and enjoy. It does not matter in any way whatsoever, whatever it is that I choose to think about, in whatever manner I choose to think, this is my experience.

Hence, if a plant as me thinks of the most perfect environment, that is my choice and experience. Believe it or not! If a plant thinks of itself as an airbreathing plant which takes in all of its apparent nutrient from the air, it will be so done and it will exist in an atmosphere which is salubrious for this.

For the joy of experimentation, look at the surface of the globe. All over the earth's surface are hospitable and inhospitable climates. Yet in each climate bacteria, suborder plants, plants of a great variety, all live and proliferate in great magnitude. It is an exciting adventure to watch. As well as the socalled lower order of life forms, many higher order of life forms choose—get the word here **choose**—to live in these various environmental zones not encouraging to life forms, including the ocean depths and the depths of the Earth and the atmosphere and above!

Who then is there who can say yea or nay to anything as to its beneficial utility in supporting life and providing a zone in which existence chooses to express.

I am always there, me, god, creating and expressing, and being myself in my myriad ways for the joy of it, for the opportunity of being me. I have no higher calling than to be and express my IS and the IS that is.

Who is there, then, that can say what is right or wrong, good or bad, beneficial or nonbeneficial, delightful or sad! All just is and always will be and exists as illusions. Since these illusions are meaningless and judgmentaless and unconditionaless, where is the practical response which says it is morally right or wrong, good or bad.

I am not talking about social-interpersonal-morals. This should be clear in all discussions relative to god. God is amoral socially. God does not judge. God places no conditions on any of its creation. God does not possess itself—its creation. God does not place any importance on illusions in any way, shape or form. If I for one moment think of me as judging anything I would be calling myself to task for what I create and do and I am incapable of doing anything to myself (my creation) which is contrary to my choice. All is my choice!

I, as the plant, do everything to myself—which might be judged good, bad or indifferent—and I do that which I do because I am the one doing and the one receiving the doing. This is such a simple response it would seem that all my creation would recognize this instantly as me in their thinking system. Albeit, some like to create a world in which problems dwell, in which challenges are the rule of the day, in which one day negative and the next day positive events take place.

Again . . .

Yes, the plant thinks.

The plant determines its environment.

The plant determines which environment it will inhabit.

Yes, plants in arid climates are there by choice. It could be said by some there is a greater power in the universe than the expressions themselves acting as me in themselves in me. There is always and only me everywhere in everything as everything. That is all.

All For The Fun Of It

Why would plant or animal or man ever choose any environment less than habitable to its highest expression—**for the fun of it!** Really, for the fun of it! Could there be any other reason. Surely not!

I never make a mistake. Some take pleasure in saying god MADE a mistake here. Not I! I do everything for the fun of it and I always will do everything for the joy of it and it is wonderful to be just this way.

From the objective point of view of humanity, those reading these words, it is obvious that many, if not plants alone including humans, would surely not choose to live in poverty and limitations of various natures. Well, be assured, I, as god, say they do make the choice and are making it daily. Regardless of what anyone would ever say, they are all living where they are living, doing what they are doing, experiencing what they are experiencing for the sole purpose of doing what they choose to do, all as me. No other purpose save that one alone.

Stand firm in the awareness that plants think, plants act, plants transfer themselves as me from one corner of the world to the other and around again at my choice, by letting my spore fly through the air, seeds be eaten by birds, and by hundreds of other possibilities and thence to occupy that new location, locations!

There is nothing in life that takes place by chance.

Everything is done purposefully and yet without purpose, only for the fun of it.

As every plant expresses itself fully and well at every turn of the Sun, so its environment is enjoyed fully and well and so is its relationship to itself, its neighbor, its atmosphere and ME. For I am each plant, I am all plants, I am the individual and I am the universal. I am the allness of all and the uniqueness of the unique.

When the bard says *a tree is a tree is a tree is a tree, by any other name, a tree is a tree,* his meaning is clear. All is god. Call god a rose, a tree, an animal, a person, a galaxy, a universe or whatever I will, it is always god.

So I may call any of my creation by various names, but all of the time my creation is me and I am my creation. My creation is the expression of my allness and yet expresses only a small portion of the allness which I am. It does not change the possibility that the plant is always able to be all which I am should that ever occur *to it* to do that.

Ignorance of reality does not change reality.

I am all even while I am expressing as one tree, one plant, one animal, one human being, or one of a host of beings, or most, or all—I am always all!

∞

4

I AM A CONCEPT

Whatever I want to think for myself I am.

I am the total freedom of expression in the infinite role of my imagination. I am every thought that ever will be thought, every thought that ever was thought, and every thought that is at this instant being thought.

I am both materialized and visualized.

Everything that I enter in my thinking system I fulfill. I thoroughly delight myself in playing the games of variety and uniqueness.

Since every thought ever considered already exists as a fulfilled expression, for me to participate in the effect of any cause all I do is to think the thought and it is manifest. For me to enjoy any idea, regardless how amazing and unrealistic, all I do is think the idea and out of the undifferentiated matter of all that idea stands forth revealed in all its glory and beauty.

Out of the infinite storehouse of ideas stands every possibility for the enthusiasm I have for myself. I can imagine the most improbable circumstance or thing ever dreamed and because I have dreamed it, that which I dream comes forth. There is nothing that tells me that whatever it is that I can visualize, imagine, dream or conceive that will be withheld from my experience.

It is not just because I am god that this is true.

It is because **all exists and all awaits my thought to manifest**.

It is the same with all of my creation.

Should a stone think (and right now each reading this is thinking, how can a stone think, how can a stone have an idea other than that of itself—and by virtue of thinking that a stone can think of the idea of itself the realization comes that a stone indeed thinks—and think it does) it can imagine itself anything which it chooses. Should any of my creation "think" my creation can visualize themselves in any way whatsoever which might be something of interest to them, this is exactly what is accomplished.

Even as I think, so all of my creation as me also think, and as I think outlandish, fantastic and heretofore apparently unthought of thoughts, so does each of my creation. My creation is me in every sense of the word. My creation is a concept, even as I am a concept whenever I think of myself as a concept.

The reason, actually, that I never think of myself as a concept or as an individualistic presentation of anything, is that should I ever do this I am this and while being this I do not encompass the whole which I am—even while encompassing that whole.

How Great Am I

As I write my autobiography I remain close to the reality which I am. Doing this I would say nothing. I would be nothing. I would say everything and I would be everything.

From my point of view I am everything and always will be everything. Being this I am all and am uninterested in being any finite aspect of my allness.

However, from the point of view of my creation, each one created to be an aspect of my allness, being a finite expression and being it to its ultimate capacity is the design for which each is created. To not think of each of my creation, created to respond to the parameters about which I have encompassed them, would be ludicrous.

A tree is created to be a tree. A house is created to be a house. An animal is created to be an animal. And MAN is created to be most like my own total self albeit expressing one level at a time, one point of consciousness right now and living one life in the present tense.

While each has the innate reality of being all, the role, the game, the choice is to pretend each is ONLY whatever it seems to be outpicturing at the present moment. Forgetting its allness and its reality as purely a concept in the cosmic realm, able to know and be all should it choose to be.

The problem with being all is that I am not conscious of being any finite aspect of my infiniteness.

I know just how great I am when I do not know my finiteness, when I am my finiteness but do it just as I live in my body.

The Intricate Body, Man

Man lives in a human body. This body is composed of an infinite number of cells each having a complex network of protoplasm, usually with a nucleus, cytoplasm and an enclosing membrane. All plants and animals are made up of one or more cells that usually combine to form various tissues. To function, these cells are surrounded by neutrons acting as a nervous system with its nerve cell body and processes including an axon and one or more dendrites.

However, for my creation man, I have created a host of complex programs with which it functions. The 100,000 chemical reactions which occur in the brain every second require intensive amounts of energy which must be fed to it by its host body. The brain utilizes as many calories in intense concentration as do the muscles of the body during heavy exercise. For this reason when a man thinks he becomes as exhausted as though he were exercising heavily.

Interestingly enough the brain has no nerve endings to sense pain or pleasure. In prehistoric times operations were done on the brain of patients who survived because of this fact. Without sensation the brain may be burned, frozen or cut.

It is reported: one square inch of human skin contains some 20 million cells, 620 sweat glands, 65 hairs, 20 feet of blood vessels, 20,000 sensory cells and also 20 million microscopic animals, such as the ubiquitous mite.

In all, the body replaces itself completely monthly shedding dead skin cells, replacing them with new skin cells.

Man does not consciously direct the activities of the flow of blood through the veins and arteries and capillaries. He allows it to take place. He does not realize that his brain is interpreting the sensations from within and without his body and forming judgments as to how the entire body should respond to any one sensation. He is unaware of the technique his brain utilizes in receiving pictures from the outside world, processing them through the lens of the eyes, determining what, if any, action should result from the observations made by the eyes. He hears sounds by the score and must interpret them and determine if any are threatening, soothing, rememberable, or informative in a useful pattern for his daily activity. And these are but a few of the obvious activities, more include: heart, lungs, organs, walking, thinking, singing, digestion, elimination, assimilation, etc. A never ending list accrues.

This same procedure is utilized by the infinite being infinite to conduct finite processes in a finite way and yet remain infinite.

Thus the term "concept" evolves without relative persuasion.

Things just are and remain so without considering an otherness. For to be aware of anotherness would defeat the universal quality of my godself.

I Am Concept—ALL!

The body might be similarly thought of in this stead.

Should I ever think that I am my hand, I am limited to the hand separated from the body. Should I think of myself as being my aching foot, I am limited to being my foot with its aches and pains and being separated from the entire salubrious body.

A small point of conjecture, but a monumental touch of awareness.

I am everything. I am nothing. I am allness. I am nothingness. Regardless where my consciousness may be at any instant, I am always all that I am, even while thinking I am not all which I am.

Though I might think of myself as THE HAND at the same moment I am the WHOLE BODY and can never be separated from it. Even, heaven forbid, if my hand were separated from the body, it would still be my hand and the hand of the whole body in question.

I can readily understand this from the abstract point of view, but when it gets down to the practical or applied condition, therein the theoretical remains aloof from my practical awareness. Just as I say two times two equals four, it is meaningless because it is just a theory for which I have no practical understanding. To tell myself I know how my body functions is equally ludicrous. I just do not know and I will never know because sincerely I have no interest in knowing that series of facts.

I think I am interested in knowing why the sky is blue, why the oceans recycle themselves, why plants grow, why clouds form, why babies are born, why I die, why I am able to see and talk and listen and taste and touch and all sorts of other possible conjectures—concepts—which seemingly are of interest to me. Actually I am not at all interested. Peripherally I have a casual questioning, but not an interest which will cause me to probe deeply. Even when I can read it in a scientific journal, a popular publication, hear it on radio or see it on television, I smile and say, "Ah so!" and let it go at that. To make it part of my memorabilia of information by learning it and comprehending fully what is being told, this takes too much attention and is just trivia information at best—when would I ever actually have a need for that knowledge. With this same interest I think about the hundreds of ramifications of my infinite self and my relative self—I just do not care.

I, as the divine, the I am within each of my creation cause such a condition to exist in the thinking system because it is a part of the package of rules of the game called being a human being.

In writing the game plan for being a human being, the concept that it does not know, cannot know, and does not really want to know, are paramount in the thinking system. So long as this parameter of the game persists, the desire to be fully aware will never surface.

From my divine self, I know and I am known. Actually in the same consciousness which my creation have indeed to an extent it might be considered that I have the same consciousness.

Just as when the millipede was asked how it directed its many legs to walk, when the millipede thought about it, it was unable to walk.

So if man asked himself how he breathed and with studied need he sought out the answer, in the process, very likely, he would forget how to breathe. Naturally this presumes that the man is REALLY INTERESTED in knowing all about breathing. If, with the normal cursory abandon, man studies breathing, he will be utterly undisturbed by the art and science of breathing.

Onepointed Dedication

All creation has the capacity to know all. I am all. I know all. I am all creation. I am god. I am me. I am interested in all. I am uninterested in all. I exist.

The ability to think one thought and experience that one thought is a normal experience for humanity. Mankind does this an infinite number of times daily but is unaware that he is doing it because he thinks the thought, visualizes the idea, accepts the concept, and it is completed.

If this were not true, my creation would not exist. Existence calls for being onepointed and having the autonomic nervous system of the body respond to the subliminal thoughts which cause it to do those things which must be done instantly to maintain and sustain the body in harmony with its world—both the body within and the body without. I "feel" "think" warm and my blood vessels constrict; I "feel" "think" cool or cold and my blood vessels dilate. Can man conceive that he causes the thought process to initiate such complex procedures as the constricting or dilating of blood vessels and arteries, capillaries and nervous system vessels—all responsive to our intuitional and sometimes physical or determined thought choices.

My thought system is based upon billions of brain neurons which are in constant active firing sending signals to and from various parts of my body, whose signals bring specific responses and which trigger responses from other areas of the body and mind.

The complexity of the human body, the human brain, the human system which responds to its environment and its interpersonal relationships is beyond comprehension by man itself. It can be comprehended. It is not comprehended because it is so complex.

Man chooses to study his environment and inner and outer space of his planet, rather than do research meaningfully on his own inner self. The inner self is not simple physiology but psychology dealing with mystical realms, psychic interpretations, metaphysical awareness, interpersonalrelationships and interpsychicalrelationships, as well as interhumananimalnonhumanrelationships. These are just the obvious relationships. These are just the expected and projected contextual interactions that must be faced by humanity in dealing with himself and the world at large.

This gives a slight idea why mankind feels so insufficient in his dealing with these relationships and in his encountering them even while fully not understanding any one phase much less the interaction of the many phases all compounded together.

With onepointed dedication understanding may be realized. If it is realized then the confusion may again compound itself because the results of such findings demand even further interactions.

To study the outer world, my creation for man and his creation for himself, is far more reasonable and effective than this inner step into a cosmic potpourri not yet trod by human society.

I am the concept.

As the concept I am free to wander into any area of self and to fully understand that which I have sought to understand. Therein, while understanding, I will also be able to no longer **need** to know the reasons for all things being—however at the same time, I will know all things and why they are the way they are, but it will no longer be of interest to me.

Potpourri—My Anthology

The melody or miscellany of my personality is beyond compass and though it is truly my anthology, the potpourri of my expression, it is just one step in the everlasting path of my reflection.

Since this mixture of my essence leading to only one aspect of my beingness is in itself infinite, and since I have an infinite number of aspects to my being, no anthology will ever be complete which merely reflects the interest of the compiler—me—in the areas of my interest.

Who am I as a concept: I am life; I am love; I am humanity; I am purity; I am vegetable; I am mineral: I am that which I am.

Does this bring me any closer to understanding who and what I am; nevermore. Does this allow humanity to be anymore aware of the inward path than it had at any previous moment in time; hardly. Does this relieve me and the universe in which I dwell from the responsibility of taking full charge of my life and affairs: it could not be that way.

At all times I am the master of my life and my expression.

At all times I am the one which chooses the pathway for which I have chosen to live in this lifetime.

The mystery which lay before me as mankind is not insoluble, but rather one which is a challenge and a funfilled adventure of searching and finding, revealing and reveling in the truth so revealed. I stand at the threshold of all wisdom and begin to open my eyes to the beauty and revelation of all which forcefully faces me at this juncture of my universe.

I am a concept.

Truly I am every concept.

I am all.

I am. ∞

5

I AM FORM

I let my imagination expand to its greatest and most imaginative scope to fulfill the cosmic creativity for which I am legend. I have the entire reach of thought over which to dream and form the ideas of my consciousness. I am unlimited and so is the form which floods forth out of my thinking system.

The thought that there is nothing new under the Sun intimates that regardless of how the imagination vaunts itself into the seemingly unknown, whatever it conceives of itself thinking has in the infinite storehouse of expression already been expressed, already been conjoined one idea with the other to form expressions of great imagination.

This in no way hampers the possibilities and remarkabilities of the formation of ideas. Even though in the realm of infinite ideas all of the ideas ever thought and to be thought exist in specifics and uniqueness.

This is likened to a storehouse with millions of arms, millions of legs, millions of hands-feet-toes-fingers-heads-specific areas of the body, all awaiting being gathered into one form or many forms.

Just as a child reaches into his Lego box of parts and creates his imaginative vehicles, people, forms without number, and even through what he brings forth, there are only so many metamorphoses and all have been tried at one time or another, albeit they are new to the child and to me.

This same process enlivens me as I consider the variations of my thought, the mutations of my form and how I may form anything. In my awareness, I may not realize that at some point in my being I have made every possible permutation an idea may express within its own field. However, this is not the last or even the beginning of its transformations.

I can add other sets of Lego blocks to the series which I have been playing with and increase my number of choices. Then when I add something to the field which is totally inconsequential to what is thought usual or normal, the possibilities stretch out again into such a variety of new form possibilities, my imagination takes flight in directions unthought of previously.

This spectacular journey into the possible and undreamed of illumines the panorama of forms available to expression.

Imagination Without End

Creative consciousness likes to dwell on the norm. What has been done and what is being done and what could be done working from any given substructure.

The truly delightful realm of unreasonableness is when, as the child, I do the unexpected, I put things together that **do not belong together,** for as I do this I step outside the usual and visit the unthought of, the unheard of, the unimagined, and when I do this, miracles take place, magic results and I am amazed.

The amazement should not be there, for the possibilities have always been open to me to experience, I have just not reached out of the fundamental formness which has been my heritage from the beginning of my awareness.

Science fiction writers love to dwell on this plane and come forth with what are considered monsters and unconscionably ugly beings. Monsters because I am not accustomed to them; ugly because I have too small a definition for beauty.

I want to like the unlikeable.

The reason I want to like that which is different is that from time to time I experience that which is unusual to me and I do not want to miss the blessing which comes from broadening my vista of life and sharing.

Walt Disney characterized this in a cartoon *Beauty and the Beast* **which is a fable** about a very ugly being who entrances a princess and in turn is beloved by all.

This is not an unusual story. It is told time and again by humanity for itself. The ugly ducklings is another such theme which points out the goose egg raised by ducks is incongruous with its peers until it is realized that the gosling is indeed an enchanting goose and not a duck.

The witch's tale tells of the princess who kisses a frog which magically turns into a prince.

The mind of mankind wants to have an opportunity to be bigger than what his society and civilization expect of him. Whenever he does this he feels ten feet tall and mighty wonderful.

Playing the game of imagination without end places everyone on the magical level of creator, expressing unimagined dreams. Forms await my touch. My gifted are searching and probing into the realm of dreams to fashion the mystic wisdom which has no bounds. It is up to the thoughtfulness of each thinker to combine in infinite selections the forms and phases of the Lego creations—which more truly are the archetypal reality revealing itself.

I am all form.

Every possible form that could ever be conceived or that ever has or is expressed is out of the creative imagination of my mind.

As a human I love to play the game of creative form.

As a human, and I must think like a human to express in human form, I present myself with the normal, and usual, and with the unusual. The unusual might be considered the sideshow freaks of yesteryear who amazed people coming to view those whose deformity was likened to a child gone wild with his Lego building system.

Every
I Am Any‸Form

Broadly speaking I can float over the panorama of creation.

From a more candid and understandable level of thinking, it is wise to think for a moment of how this creation of form takes place. This can be considered with anything, but for the moment I will consider a human being.

There is an archetypal design which establishes what a human being is and how it should act and how it should conduct itself.

Strangely enough few human beings have taken **any** time to even think about the system by which the design functions. Every design—to achieve its design and function—has specific parameters and end result affects. These are created basically for humans and are easily known. Too often with a childish libertine action I create the physical bodies in which I live and in the process have brought forth something less than the original design would suggest.

A new parent so often thinks "will my child be whole and perfect" and in this very act of thinking imagines something which is considered "not perfect" and hence that is the creation placed in motion to be an effect in the body of the newborn.

This misinformed form which could be so easily formed one way or another is done through the lack of onepointedness in the thought system. It is such a specific project.

As for myself, god, I have no problems here.

I create myself and all of my creation exactly as the whim catches me or as my imagination strikes me.

However, for me and my thoughtful creation, I first establish a "design" and follow that plan to its completion and therein my creation are the exact replica of my blueprint for them. Of course, I am onepointed. I think one thought and take it from MY CHOICE of design to MY CHOICE of fulfillment or manifested form. With my pure attitude toward each of my creation I remain consistent and what I reap is what I sow—which is always true even with those who seemingly create with diversity. They too get what they create in great variety and complexity.

Why does it not matter whether the grand design is followed or not; why is it inconsequential whether an apparent malformation results or whether the grand scheme is fulfilled; why is the child libertine with its Lego blocks at liberty to create as he chooses when it is apparent that this was not the first plan or thought?

Reality Is The Design, Illusion Is Unreality

Form comes and goes as an illusion. Form is without permanency. Only the design from which the form manifests is the reality. Only the pattern, the archetypal picture stands firm and resolute through an infinite number of apparent misunderstood uses of its desired effect.

No design or pattern is better than another. Each pattern is used to fulfill "a purpose" and that is exactly what it does.

As a seamstress selects a pattern for a dress. She adjusts the perfect pattern for the variable shape of the customer. She adjusts the fabrics for the choice of the customer. She adjusts the hem length to be practical for the customer. The imperfect customer wants the perfect pattern to be changed to meet her particular needs. The design is not imperfect. The seamstress or creator is not imperfect. The materials, basically, are not imperfect. The design can only be followed or modified to fit a particular desire of the one who uses it. The closer one remains with the pattern, the more perfectly the results are reflected by the model or prototype.

The universe is filled with perfect designs.

The cosmos vibrates to the harmony of perfection.

It is only when I the viewer choose to observe imperfection or inharmony, only because of my viewpoint, that I experience this lack of symmetry and balance, reflection of the perfect design.

As the creator returns to the original archetypal picture then does the perfect outline reveal itself and only then is the perfect picture given to the universe of the absolute within it.

The perfect pattern, this is the same as the concept *to heal* in the dictionary: *return to my original perfection and integrity,* requires that I "fit" in the pattern, that I "cooperate" with the form which I visualize for myself and for my creation. This is not something which is difficult to accomplish, it merely takes a point of view free from human objectivity.

So often I think that "this is the way things are" and I am bound to those experiences and there is nothing I can do to escape from the causes which are placed into motion.

This is incorrect.

I can establish an entirely new attitude for myself. I do not have to be oddly patterned to fit into a design. I can be the perfect design and fit into the mold as well. This is done as I place the thought perfectly into my consciousness that I am that which I am and never shall go away from it.

This attitude demands discipline and dedication. It is all too easy to fall into the habit of confusion and futility, thinking that there is no out for me, I just have to flow with the thinking of humanity—race consciousness—which must have its sway.

Needless to say, I am not bound by any outward conditions which would limit me and which would tell me that I am anything other than my pure unlimited nature at all times.

To be this pure and unlimited nature at times requires that I look onepointedly at what my choice is. Just what is my choice. Do I feel sorry for myself or do I know what I am and demand it be brought forth in my experience.

I as god, the infinite one, each time I claim my I AM, I walk perfectly in the way of my choice. I walk perfectly in the way of my onepointedness and "get" every effect which I am.

I have no problems getting my creation realized as the perfect divine pattern which I have established for them.

I have no problem realizing the fulfillment of my pattern in form.

I remain resolute and absolute under all circumstances.

The Form I Am

In a joyous expression of the purity of my reality I do not think of the form I would see expressed: I AM THE FORM I EXPRESS!

In the perfect realization of the pattern I devise to open the cosmic mirror of my mind, it is revealed and: I AM THE FORM I EXPRESS!

No matter the infinite examples of designs, patterns, archetypal modalities, at all times the prototype form, the original expression of it is available for manifestation in a visible form to my creation. The form awaits the conviction of its creator.

The form exists in the storehouse of all designs. The "pattern room" stands filled to overflowing with possibilities for being granted continuity and action in the physical universe.

As god I am pure idea.

I am concept.

I am undifferentiated matter.

I am form in consciousness.

I am form in illusion.

As illusion, any form which I am exists so long as it is given thought. Whenever I as form am not considered I fade into the native nothingness out of which I am born. My reality is in the concept of myself as a pattern, myself as the archetypal of my diversity, the unimagined wholeness of myself.

For illustration:

I am the archetypal tree. I am its definition and its pattern.

I am the archetypal man. I am its purest design and function. I am the prototype man in thought whose purpose is to express me in my infinitude. I am what man conceives himself to be when he closes his eyes and looks upon the screen of his consciousness for who I am.

I am the perfect archetypal house. Whatever is thought when I think of house is what "a" house is! It is its diversity of purposes as a shelter, a center of love for a family, an activity center for a family, a castle for all of its inhabitants—and in all of this it is truly formless.

I am the archetypal airplane or automobile. I am its definition and its purpose. The perfect outer form is not yet available to current man—me—only because I have not taken time to question the inner self as to just what the perfect vehicle is and how it looks.

I am the archetypal world or planet Earth. As the perfect prototype of my game place for my created humanity it is created to change with its needs and evolutionary use. This is the pattern which I have established to be varied and unique for its enjoyment.

I am the archetypal "heaven" wherein humanity chooses to live in harmony with itself and in harmony with its creative cause. I am the perfect expression of all that this suggests. I am that which I am and always will be that.

This is the story of what makes me what I am and forevermore I am form. I am form complete and dreamed. I am form imagined and revealed. I am form wished for and form upheld.

I am form. ∞

6

I AM CHAOS

I am chaos.

I am defined as the disorder of formless matter and infinite space, supposed to have existed before the ordered universe. Also, chaos is defined as extreme confusion or disorder and an abyss or chasm, the primeval void or chaos before creation. Truly this is that which I am, my reality, formless and infinite space.

From the human point of view I am order.

Modern day scientists have created a new discipline entitled: CHAOS. This discipline looks at random experiences of splashing water, snowflakes, evolution of planets, revolution of planetary and solar systems, and in all this and much more, find a definite order and syncronicity, a synergy marvelously revealed out of its apparent randomness. The simultaneous occurrences, rather than being nonconnected and dispart, combine in a cooperative force to reveal unique and unimagined patterns. In this synergism the simultaneous action of these apparent separate agencies, which together have a greater total effect than the sum of their individual effects, create a dynamic picture of a synthesis which each alone could never express.

What appears to be chaos to a finite objective viewer, looked at from an infinite point of view—from a much broader scope—is shown to be a wedding of concepts, conditions, objects and patterns cosmic in both breath and purpose.

Still in all of this objectified awareness of the greater realm in which the game is being played, the purpose of my game for myself is to be myself and have fun in so doing.

Cosmic Evolution

Could humanity imagine itself as a giant with the playground of the cosmos, and most importantly, anything it did or did not do were absolutely unimportant. No morality ruled its movement and action. No beneficial or unbeneficial action resulted from the effect of its apparently indiscriminate—random and promiscuous—choices! Indeed, such an apparently undisciplined approach to existing creation and new creation would be unprincipled in the eyes of humanity living in its proper illusionary world.

Haughtily the evolution of the Earth takes place.

Contrary to the prayers of humanity that its God not forget it and destroy it under the "acts of God" such as hurricanes, volcanoes, earthquakes, fire, flood and more, these apparent acts of God do indeed take place with a seeming vengeance.

But do they take place with a revenge punishment for those involved in a way that seems totally without redemption to those suffering through it. Such venial action from the creator had to be excusable and did not destroy the spiritual being of those involved, so it seems.

But imagine, since I am so grand that the cosmos is indeed my playground in which I may do anything I choose without censure, where is any restraint?

The hurricane devastates the lives of thousands, perhaps more, and destroys property valued at billions of dollars—all apparently thoughtlessly.

The volcano erupts sending forth geysers of lava, water and steam, inundating villages, cities and countrysides wherein people live and have their livelihood all wiped out indiscriminately, seemingly quite unfair to the inhabitants therein. The voluminous ubiquitous ash soars into the heavens and darkens the skies forming a greenhouse effect overwhelming all the nations on Earth. To what purpose? Certainly, apparently, not to the benefit of those living at that time and in those places.

As the great tectonic plates which form the crust of the Earth change, rising and falling, slipping and sliding, with no apparent direction and purpose, cities are swallowed up and lives are lost and values are devastated by such a "disaster."

Interestingly, humanity cooperates significantly with this cosmic game by choice, building its cities over seismic faults on the crust of the globe, knowing full well earthquakes take place there, and it is only a matter of time until it will happen again.

Humanity chooses to live on the slopes and in the valleys of known volcanoes, where their ancestors had lived for centuries, knowing the great "God volcano" would definitely erupt again and again over the years.

Twenty-first century civilized human beings in major countries of the world build their homes in forested regions subject to fires. They know that fire protection is taught to them to keep a firebreak thirty feet out from their houses, build houses with fire retardant roofs, keep adequate water available to wet down their structures in case of impending fire, and avoid certain types of structures because fire damage is most severe for that type of structure—in all these *humans choose purposefully to build and live in jeopardy.*

Homes are built in flood basins, flood plains, below dams, in a variety of places subject to flooding—purposefully—throughout history.

Seashore homes are built even as the tide washes away the cliffs and sand spits on which they are constructed. Families build in the onslaught of warring nations knowing their danger, polluted areas and cities attract those who would work there regardless of the danger to the health of their family, and the list continues showing that purposefully humanity is careless of its own welfare, to a large extent. In other words, the desire to put themself in peril seems to be part of human nature. Why exposure to danger thrills humanity would be difficult to explain if we did not know of the fragile quality of the illusion mankind lives and truly know that it is not his reality.

Cosmic Man

Because man can conceive the cosmic pattern of an infinite creator, perhaps not completely at this moment, but even in a small way, man begins to enjoy the universe as a whole and in this vast and grandiose vision sees the humor of having fun with the infinite. The seriousness of how things "must be" fades into the game.

As a child stands beside rain puddles with water running from one to the other he makes little dams, and with sticks and leaves for boats, he cruises from one lake to another. He indiscriminately builds dams between the lakes, he redirects water from one area to an area of his choice. He thinks it would be fun to jump up into the air and come splashing down in the middle of one of his lakes causing water to storm over his domain. He abandons his game when supper is called and more rain carelessly washes out the lakes, the boats, and dams and the rivers between them. The child returns later to see all is washed away, the storm is over and there are no more water puddles in which to play his game. He turns his attention to a new adventure, absolutely forgetting the old game which had been so much fun until the evolution of the day and the rain and the Sun brought change into his life as it constantly does moment by moment.

I am this cosmic child, cosmic man, playing my game with abandon and joy, with no responsibility but a choice to be unique, imaginative and always changing, never stable or consistent. I just am myself and have fun being that which I am.

What a chaos results from the child jumping in the puddle of water where each drop spreads to foreign spots, some melding with mud or dust, others rinsing dust from objects, the lake emptied, the river gutted, the "boats" lakeless high and dry on distant shores, all so thoughtless and purposeless.

If I could see from a viewpoint yet higher than that of the child I could understand a broader pattern of order which seemingly is lost in this "local" experience.

Chaos is all about me. Chaos is the foundation of life. Chaos is the movement of lymph fluid through my body, blood coursing through my arteries and veins, food entering the digestive chain, elimination of empty energy carriers, the breath I intake, the words I speak or hear, the way I walk or travel, all the act of a chaotic pattern—albeit, within that pattern is order unknown on my finite screen.

I, as god, know this about myself and my creation and I like it just that way.

The "purpose" if any purpose there be, for any creation to exist, is to be itself, whatever that self is conceived to be, and to have fun being that self as they conceive it to be.

Just as I lie in smiling repose attending to the experiences my creation as me is having, so I do so without judgment, for I could never judge any action which I undertake and call it anything but good and very good. I thoroughly love the diversity and disparity of incongruity which living in a chaotic environment produces. Even more, the careless attitude of my creation being me in their own marvelous ways is something which brings delight to my being.

What to an ersatz orderly society is valued as worthy, the real order is overlooked in favor of a temporary appearance.

I Am My Creation

While the human child looms massively over his finite universe, I, being infinite, for illustration sake, loom over my either infinite or finite universe, and have fun being me.

Again for illustration sake:

The globe on which mankind dwells called Earth is a composite of various levels of structure.

There is the outer layers of the stratosphere, tropopause, the atmosphere, the layer of earth-rock-and ground on which humanity live, the sublayers of the Earth including its tectonic plates, the magma—liquid or molten rock deep in the earth, and other core substances.

For me it is the pattern of evolution which I have put into motion for the globe to change its surface often lifting and lowering the ocean, having ice ages, warm ages, a variety of creatures on Earth ever changing with the climate and circumstances of the crust or surface of the globe. All this is a broader view which I see of the Earth unfolding my pattern for it.

For one unaware it might seem that I am moving directionlessly in my development of the Earth. This is quite true and with it are the millions of possibilities which I can utilize in unfolding my image for the world. Any age, changing landscape, changing population in its diverse form, always changing, my joy.

There is truly nothing new in the universe, in the allness of all, so everything I choose to do, in its diverse and multiple ways has been done and will be done again and again over eons of time. Whatever my imagination can dream will result in an action expressed in my creation.

One moment I may have the tectonic plates erase all that has ever gone before and humanity with its sacred archeology will say categorically that no life existed before a specific time. They are so limited in their thinking! How often have the surface plates of the planet changed and re-changed and changed again, moving all trace of prior civilizations and living creatures from view so that it appears they never were there in the first place.

Actually I have created an infinite number of civilizations upon the face of the Earth over millions of years. Over these millions and billions of years the plates have obliterated all reference to previous expressions—in their diverse forms, often quite contrary to what humanity might find usual in this day of an oxygen rich atmosphere. At times the atmosphere was not thus and the creatures living then breathed quite differently, their "needs" were quite unique by today's standards, and their way of living would seem strange indeed by Twenty-First Century ways.

Since I am god I can do anything that I choose.

There are no laws or Law of cause and effect defining how things shall be brought forth out of the infinite awareness. Since all things are, were and always have been, evolution per se is a rather limited concept of how things come to be.

Humanity loves to look at the story of history as laid out on the layers of rock and soil depicting the span of one culture's existence thinking that this was the only time in history that particular culture expressed in just that way having evolved from a specific to a specific expression unique and alone in that point of evolutionary time. Not so! I am not bound by ages or times, by evidence and nonevidence. I am able, at any point in expression, to have all express in a specific way or in a multispecific way which mankind would say had never been. For instance, should I choose, I can combine the period of 1995 with year 1 and have both coexist harmoniously and not seem intrusive or unique to that expression.

Humanity does not find it unusual that all of the modern conveniences exist in modern cities and not in rural areas. Also it is not unusual that rural areas do not know of the available richness of the city, having no television, radio, newspapers, or communication with the city so far away. The people are quite content to exist as they know they exist in deprivation, as viewed by the city brother. As I explain it here, it is perfectly logical. Were it not explained, it would seem ludicrous that such a condition exists.

View with me the larger tableau.

With "my unseen fingers" I slide the tectonic plates about on the surface of the Earth—sometimes quickly and most of the time, apparently, exceedingly slowly—and I do this for the fun of being me, just as the child jumps in the puddle and creates a world of lakes, dams and miscellanea.

Without seeming regard for the creatures living on the surface, I slide the plates higher, up and down, joyously fingering the puzzle of the globe. Just as the hurricane, flood, fire, earthquake and storms of every nature carelessly fault the residents of the place wherein they wreak their havoc, and are not thought of being humanistically unmerciful, so I take the illusions of my creation and change their status from time to time—life or death, sick or well, prosperous or devastated—and mold the world scenery, its weather, its world shaking volcanoes and earthquakes from plates moving about seemingly without purpose—and so they are purposelessly moving.

I do not do these things out of meaningful travail to those dwelling there. I do these things out of an overall—big picture—of a concept I have in mind.

From this point of view people who pray to me to make right what I have chosen to do another way are speaking spuriously, knowing full well this is contrary to MY DESIRE.

However, because all is chaos, it does not matter which direction anything would choose to express in, it would be perfectly acceptable. I do anything that I choose by choosing.

Everything I Think I Manifest

Humanity does anything it chooses by choosing also, but it has not learned to be disciplined and onepointed sufficiently to accomplish that which it seemingly desires for itself. One moment, it is so strong in its will that such happens. A moment later at some whim it changes its desire and hence the thing does not come forth. The difference between me and my creation is that I think something and it IS. I go on to an infinite number of other thinks and things, but all of the time that which I THOUGHT is manifest and is not something waiting to demonstrate.

For humanity speaks its word and then places another word on the block and says that perhaps it will not take place—and it does not take place.

Humanity does manifest its choice by not having its first choice, but rather its second-third-fourth-etc. thought revealed, or even some more distant thought.

I manifest everything I think because my thought is instantly manifested even while I am thinking it.

Long I have suggested to those would-be practitioners of spiritual healing that when I am asked for a prayer or treatment, I immediately say to the person: *You are whole and perfect!* By doing this the cause is put into motion to bring about its result. Whether the person being treated wants wholeness or not, if I am asked to treat for them, it is done. **It is done the instant I speak my word—or think my thought—or know it is done!** No further work is necessary for this project.

It is understandable that humanity would think all is chaos, when everyone has the indwelling spirit of truth and everyone is indeed god, as I have said numerous times in the great philosophical and religious teachings of every age.

So on Earth now are some six billion beings who each are god. From one point of view one would think what diversity, what unimaginable confusion, how many billions of expectations, not all harmonious with one another.

But even this is a balance, a harmony, a oneness, a peace, a togetherness which aligns all into one synchronistic community, as a great clockwork, each gear doing its own thing, necessary for the harmonious telling of time by yet other factors required of the clock if it is to fulfill its usefulness.

The diversity of the clock requires many factors:

1. A known time.
2. A rate of time.
3. A face that pictures the correct time.
4. A network of gears and ratchets and rods all functioning harmoniously to maintain a rhythm to tick off the time.
5. A power source to cause the clock to operate at a given speed.
6. Something to control and regulate the desired time.
7. Someone to need to know the time and use it for some purpose.

All these disparate uses, functions, and purposes in the working of a device to record time are absolute chaos to one another. Each seemingly has no harmonizing factor which would wed one concept to another, yet they intrinsically require one another most marvelously and perform their work synchronistically, synergistically.

To look at the cog of any one gear, or cutting off all the cogs and joining them together in one pile would be meaningless. To take the gears and randomly place them within the mechanism would bring chaotic results—albeit they would be harmonious, but not for the purpose of the clock. Putting the numbers on the face of the clock in random order would produce confusion if one were to try to tell "time" as defined by the original purpose of creating the clock.

Should the device which determines the speed at which the clock runs be faulty or not in sync with the modus operandi under which the clock is to function would bring about meaningless time for the clock reader.

Should the power unit which makes the clock function be in any way not functioning at its proper strength and continuity, the moment by moment, hour by hour, minute by minute, second by second, millisecond by millisecond, and even more finite fractional time would cease to have its accuracy so necessary for the telling of time.

To any observer looking at a clockworks the obvious chaos would be seen in abundance immediately. For to the untrained eye, all that is not known to it appears as confusion and disparity. To anyone who sees the randomness of life, its confusion would cause that one to say, *it is but worthless direction and without purpose.*

All through history all who viewed the snow falling thought it was all the same pattern which each flake depicted until some enterprising painstaking scientist looked at each snowflake they were able to maintain in its "cold pattern" to find that each was indeed different. Some magical *differentiating system* was making every pattern unique and beautiful—why and how—a mystery, but not a mystery to that which created the differentiation.

Confusion is never confusion to one who knows and finds order in all things. The order in all things comes out of the recognition that while nothing needs to have a purpose, nothing needs to have a reason for being, all things do have such a reason—and that reason is just to be itself and have fun.

Chaos is its own reason for existence.

With the improved systems of science today to investigate the chaos of the universe, they are finding that really nothing is in absolute chaos, meaning confusion. There is order everywhere and that order is based on a patterned functional harmony one with the other in manners in which all may not be privy, but all can know should they choose to listen to me within telling the reality of all.

Indeed, I am chaos!

I am the randomness and the confusion of all. But even in this randomness and apparent confusion I am at the center of it. I am the binding love, the glue which unites all in the activity of love and oneness.

As with the clockwork, to the uninitiated it would appear to be a vast network of metal shaped oddly and ineffectively, but in the last analysis, it is a lovely clock functioning to its own end.

As the child playing in the mud, stomping in the puddles, and pretending he has ships, lakes, rivers, and a vast tidal wave I selfcreated by my marvelous leap, so I am constantly creating my own magical world of uniqueness, purposelessness and interest to basically myself alone. For everyone of my creation have the same quality of creative genius within them and display it as uniquely as the other—and wonderfully, like the snowflake, each is sincerely different from one another.

Though I may fondle the Earth and slip its tectonic plates this way and that to my delight and creative imagination, all is done out of love for myself. Though it may appear that my creation are done-in by the creative efforts I express, in truth they are not. There is no life, there is no death, there is no experience at one place of the universe or the other, there is only being myself and having fun.

As I ride the roller coaster for the thrill and fun of it, so I build my home over the earthquake fault, on the edge of the ocean which is at this very moment undermining it, in the path of a volcano's action-flood-fire or a thousand disasters. It is not I who present these mystical magical thrill-a-minute experiences for my creation but my creation themselves. They love it. I love it too. I love life and I love living.

The appearance of chaos is only an appearance. All is more orderly than is presently known. But in the research being done all that which appears confusion now, will be seen for just what it is in the very near future—an orderly pattern of the most marvelous being.

- ❑ True, we see with local vision.
- ❑ True, the world is now seen via satellite.
- ❑ True, the planets are being revealed to us.
- ❑ True, the galaxies are coming closer with our telescopes and our satellites which take pictures of them.
- ❑ True, I may never see with the ultimate vision of all that is and its creative cause, this I will have to know from within myself,

that is where I as god show my creation the theater of the heart that all may be fully revealed and fully known.

Chaos—smile! ∞

7

I AM UNDIFFERENTIATED MATTER

I am the substance of the universe.

As this substance I am neither its reality, nor its insubstantiation of unreality and imaginariness—I am always both and all.

Research has shown man that each cell in the body of any human, or any other living being, has within it all of the actual and potential for the entire body in which it dwells.

The entire genetic makeup of any existence dwells in each cell which is taken from or given to that form.

Creation likes to think of itself in a uniqueness and in a differentiation that makes it special in its realm of expression. This is far from the case: since all substance has within it all that it ever will be, so within all substance is all that it is capable of being either as a unique special expression or any expression that might ever be thought into demonstratableness.

This means that out of the nothingness I, god, created all and out of this same nothingness all has come forth. Hence, to this same nothingness all goes when its expression as an objective form is completed. When an "idea" is no longer thought about it returns to its native nothingness or as humanity has liked to call it in their primate thinking: dust!

Interestingly the dictionary[1] speaks in the following manner of dust: *1. powdery earth or other matter in bits fine enough to be easily suspended in air 2. a cloud of such matter 3. confusion; turmoil 4. a) earth, especially as the place of burial b) mortal remains disintegrated or thought of as disintegrated to earth or dust 5. a humble or abject condition.*

The substance out of which creation comes forth is often called dust. In this generalized term it is understandable that it refers more to its finiteness and indefinableness than it does of its substance.

In every atom is a living moving acting and thinking center. This reality which is the substance of all sensitive and objective existence, has

---

1 Webster's New World Dictionary
Third College Edition

within it the "purpose" for which the thought has for its expression out of the creative undifferentiated substance of the universe.

Defining Uniqueness

The rare experience of defining the uniqueness of how substance coalesces resulting in a specific stone, plant or beingness is in itself a marvelous creation.

For, since in all substance—undifferentiated matter—dwells the unseen expression of a specific object, the question of how the universal information present in all essence decides to express itself in one "thing" or another is housed in the code within the matter itself.

In the infinite, which I am as god, there is no differentiation. All is One and ONE alone.

In the illusory world of humanity playing the game that what it sees is real and what it does not see is unreality, I allow this game to go on and be thought exceedingly important to my creation.

Whenever a human thinks of a house, tree, person or whatever, that is what is given coalescing form out of the infinite undifferentiated matter into whatever it is the human conceives it to be. Nothing more nor less. Whatever the human vitalizes as the reality for him and important to him, and limited by him, this is what I as the infinite give him as a temporary illusion which he may play with to his hearts content, believing it is reality, believing that what appears before him is more significant than what he does not see—and in this game I know that there is no seriousness in anything I do—for it is indeed a game being played by me as my creation.

I project the vast arena of imagination upon the screen of humanity, allowing it to feel that it has used a creative process to accomplish its desires. I allow humanity to feel that they have for the first time brought forth something which is both outstanding and unique.

Man does not demonstrate either a first time expression or a unique expression. All exist eternally and have always been in expression.

What humanity does, what any of my creation do, is to play with the infinite variety of concepts available in the allness and think to themselves, or itself, that what it has brought forth is a noble achievement for itself and for me. Now the latter is what truly amuses me. For humanity, in its humility, to think that there is anything anywhere ever that I have not already accomplished, is begging the question of just who and what I am.

If, indeed, I am the undifferentiated matter out of which all comes forth, and within ALL undifferentiated matter anywhere is all that could ever be or ever will be or ever was, then how could my creation acting as my creation ever do something that would either surprise me or improve over anything which I am or ever have done or ever will do! An impossibility.

That humanity may take at any moment it chooses and live in any way that it pleases and honorably express me in any of the thousands of ways that it provides enjoyment to my creation to do, this is his joyous choice and my satisfied acceptance of his expression.

One Man's Presence Quiet Of Inner Peace

This moment I am listening to a jazz pianist in a chapel playing his heart out in enthusiasm and thanksgiving revealing Afro-American spirituals uninhibited by technique or style, an open magnificence of his inner self. Now, with my recognition of his inner genius, his music begins to take on a more formal function and a harmony that before was chaotic, now is rhapsodic and all are joining in with singing and clapping and the chapel is vibrating with its holy power beyond human imagination.

Then, as quickly as it began, the music stops. The chapel reveals a peaceful silence and all present are invaded with a sense of overwhelming peace. One man walks into the chapel area with a conviction in his heart. That conviction is one of inner peace, a revelation of joy and love, and all in the holy place are brought under the charisma of this one man. He does not speak a word, he does not look particularly different from any of the others, but his inner power pervades the room and all are blessed by his awareness of himself.

The unique special expression of this "one man" who as god, being himself, invaded the consciousness of everyone in his presence. It was not so because he wished it to be so, it was so because that was his nature.

To define uniqueness is an unnecessary task.

All of my creation are unique because I created each one and everything to be an expression of myself being whatever they are!

In each is the absolutely SAME undifferentiated substance. And in the substance is the potential of all existence, of all appearance, of all expression of animal, mineral, vegetable or nonexpression. It matters not what would be, out of this essence all floods forth into manifest demonstration of that which I out of my infinite "storehouse of ideas" reveal as an expressed objectivity.

Humanity is made infinite through the power of my imagination. The quality of infinity is mine to enjoy anytime I choose but the capacity is used as man uses my imagination to ferret out the hidden recesses of consciousness for the magical marvelous imagery possible to be brought into expression as an IS in man's view.

Matter Is Not Reality

Humanity thinks that only that which is seen is real; only that which is composed of "matter" has substance and is therefore touchable and usable.

Man is as much subject to the flights of his fancy as I am to the importance of matter.

Humanity may watch a movie and become so engrossed in the activity of the film, I perspire, my blood pressure rises, I am fearful and most of all

I live the adventure before me as though I were in reality right there with the actors. In fact, I am right there with the actors, no more so than if I were physically standing amongst them participating in the adventure I am enjoying.

This is an easy case to cite, but also think of reading an adventure story or something being totally interested in, all time is lost and I am carried away by the activity I am absorbed in reading. It need not be only adventure. I get equally engrossed in technical writing, educational research, graphic creations, computer games, personal discussions with others, daydreaming, and infinite other mental games I play. My body surges forth to express the emotions, pulse and pressure, inspiration and expiration, cramped muscles, and anything else which might occur when physically present in any activity, only mentally enjoyed.

While an iceberg can melt leaving me viewing pure water, in my imagination an iceberg can appear before me numberless times in the strangest circumstances. It can be in the desert, it can be in a sauna, it can be in a swimming pool of warm water, and the iceberg does **not** melt. The iceberg remains as I picture it and I am its total creator. Whereas in what I like to call real life, the iceberg **must** melt to be consistent with its realm of reality. If the iceberg did not melt I would say it was false, not real, and discount its validity in my experience. However, in my imagination I visualize the iceberg doing all the things I in "real" life would say was a sham, but in my mental viewing state I find it absolutely acceptable for the iceberg to act quite unlike any iceberg I have ever known.

I can go back and experience a happening again and again in my thinking system, in my "mind" and not feel at all that this is improper. Should I seek to relive past experiences, my psychiatrist would point out to me I must move forward, that reliving the past is only in a therapy for overcoming any controlling elements of the past which limit me in the present.

My peers tell me that it is pure fantasy to live in the past because so living is not being realistic to the present.

As I review any picture of the past, I see it as it was. I may change that picture to any projection I like and I may tell myself this is the truth of the past and make it the reality of the past, never again to review the old picture which "actually" had taken place, but in its stead I hold the new image of the past and act out my present based on this "new" past.

Seems strange, yet true!

That upon which humanity bases its historical references is the information which it has in its thinking system. While whatever happened is always housed in the consciousness and will never be taken therefrom, even though a changed or new picture of history may be established upon which I base how I perceive today. In this way the past affects today and how I live today. I can, however, in reviewing the past reorganize the past to be more in keeping with my present desire for it and therein live a new now.

These remarks are given to define the quality of reality. Reality is whatever the human being desires it to be. Even that which was experienced as real in the past does not have to be that upon which preset perceptions are based in the now. From this point of view I come to the concept of the "IS."

Concept Of The IS

It does appear that humanity can completely readdress my past and my present and my future.

Should this be a reality, which indeed it is, then everything exists in a state of unbelievable fluidity. The sequence of events which give reality to man's life is not a stability at all. It is rather the taking of specific points of view and joining them to other points of view until the flux revealed is a "moving picture" of activity which is called life.

In *stop camera motion* every single frame of the camera reveals the scene in stopped action. It looks silly when the horse stands there in the process of leaping over a hedge, but I am accustomed to seeing such pictures and do not find them incredulous. However, I am skeptical when I am informed that all existence is a magnificent series of ISES flowing from one IS to another making up the cinematography of life in action.

From the cultured viewpoint humanity has not given any consideration to the concept that because of the similarity of the flow of an IS, one into another, that each IS is an IS, but rather considers the picture as a graphic whole. To think of the picture as anything other than a whole would be a travesty on the mental imagery of mankind. This has been an historic realization and universal presentation of the picture of life.

It is necessary to define just what an IS is.

An IS is the fractional segment of time that any object or thought or concept is expressing in a given wholeness, complete in itself without needing anything added to it or taken from it to understand its completeness.

This definition may not be present in any dictionary, but it is nonetheless a valid description of the reality of an IS.

Everything in life from the posit of objects or beings in their status quo, to their dance of continuity, makes these experiences come alive and be viewed under a very different set of circumstances. It makes the individual think that there certainly could never be a set of activities which would make the actions a continuation of each IS into its additional state of movement.

To be at home with the IS and the concept of how all of life as created by humanity requires an infinite number of ISes to be linked one with the other to bring about the picture of the apparent reality which I am familiar with—is both ludicrous and necessary.

Ludicrous in that my mentality finds it absurd and extremely ridiculous that such a condition should exist. This is so contrary to all of the experiences humanity has known all of its existence.

It is necessary for humanity, since that is the way it is.

Strangely enough, that is the way it is!

This is so strange and so wonderful that once humanity has grasped this awareness, it will never again believe that because something has happened it must remain a belief or an experienced reality—it can be easily and swiftly changed by linking the ISes together in a different sequence and a new reality is revealed.

Nothing is forever—save an IS which exists in perpetuity.

The cinematography of one IS with another IS reveals the great variety of change and the diversity of possibilities how undifferentiated matter may be coalesced into different forms that formerly had no relationship to one another.

Once the IS and undifferentiated matter are understood for the role each plays in the life of humanity, they can be used by mankind to be master over myself and my affairs. Until they are understood, humanity will always feel that I am subject to the wiles of an unknowable God and insofar as that is so, man will never know its innate reality.

Understanding this more fully requires that the definition of matter be given some awareness. The dictionary[2] defines matter as *what something is made of; constituent substance or material* and *what all (material) things are made of; whatever*

---

2 Ibid.

occupies space and is perceptible to the senses in some way; in modern physics, matter and energy are regarded as equivalents, mutually convertible according to Einstein's formula, $E=mc^2$ (i.e., energy equals mass multiplied by the square of the velocity of light).

This *something* of which matter is constituted is of little consequence, of great importance is that the illusion or concept of form taken by undifferentiated matter is its reality, and it is its reality to the degree and to the extent that it is taken in its onepointedness, its single observation of it at its *still motion* of the IS being itself. This *still motion* can come at any one of the thousands of IS points in its active matrix, for the pattern of its activities as well as its unique form all lie within its originating cause or divine idea. This is so compelling and demanding to every observer that if this is not respected by the viewer I am completely out of sync with the manner in which the program is being carried out for the individual unique IS.

All matter is undifferentiated, even while it is gathered into any form in which it may be used. For at all times, even while it is expressing itself as a threesome, innate in its capacity it may be a human (animal), mineral or vegetable. All possible. All probable. All potential is indwelling all matter.

Since I AM UNDIFFERENTIATED MATTER all matter is the I am. Since I am all, all undifferentiated matter is all. Since all is I am, all is all.

These statements seem to confuse reality for humanity, but once this concept is appreciated, the search into the infinite is easily and quickly accomplished. Should this awareness never be brought to mind in an individual, a civilization or a universe, its path on the way of inner understanding remains static until such time that this inner awareness is recognized.

The solution is simple but requires a new look at the concept held by most.

I.e., *if all is all then all is all and if all is all and all is all then everything is all and all is everything and nothing is all and all is nothing therefore whatever is nothing is all and whatever is all is nothing.*

Yes, I am undifferentiated matter.

All is undifferentiated matter.

Nothing is undifferentiated matter. ∞

8

ME AND MORALITY

I am always me. I am always that which I am and that which I am is fully independent of any system or rules or mode of conduct used to guide any culture in their unique development providing them with guidelines for social cooperation.

I am omnipresent. Being everywhere present and aware of peoples everywhere, who I am, I cannot judge anything which they do or think or say, since whatever they are I am. It is the individual ethics of any group which sets them aside from their brother organization. It is at such a time that one culture seeks to prompt its philosophical mien over that of its neighbor. Neither cultural program is superior to the other, save one is promoted above the other by each of the individual groups.

Decades flow into centuries and the origin of the philosophical reasoning has long been forgotten, and the manner of conducting themselves continues as an important aspect of their daily life. It becomes a code of ethics so strong that any violator is considered a heretic or pagan—not of the individual religion—of the locals.

Morality Is Right Conduct

I am more truly amoral, not to be judged by the rules or criteria of morality since my foundation dwells in every culture and in no culture. My reality includes everything and nothing. Since this is my reality, my expression, I can have no moral conformity with the local generally accepted standards of goodness or rightness in conduct or character. What is an ideal code of moral principles in one group decidedly does not fit in that of another group.

Morals are the manners and customs of a given civilization. The morality of a given group is their quality of character in how they respond to the rightness and wrongness relative to their code of conduct—such standards can never apply to a universal being, a ubiquitous expression can only be true to itself and whatever is the foundation of its own relationship to all that exist in its universe.

Even to *study* the cultures of another people, another group, leads to confusion for one seeking to live in the ultimate, the divine level of consciousness. Hence, morality is outside the scope of a universal being.

I am god. Of this there can be no doubt.

I am god in all. This translates into all being god, all being that which I am.

Since all is what I am, how does morality or right conduct relate to my actions in and through my creation, in and through humanity, and every other creation which is me—**in just one way, judgmentaless.**

Truly, this is the way—JUDGMENTALESS!

In the act of judgmentaless everything which I (all) do is good and very good. All that I think (everyone thinks) is good and very good. All that I visualize for my creation and its universe (everyone's visualization) is good and very good.

This brings to each an entirely ***new*** concept of conduct values, of what is good and bad—ipso facto—nothing is either good or bad, all exists solely for itself and its unique expression.

Let it be considered that as I speak of myself I am speaking likewise of each of my creation, of all of my creation, and thus I can flow harmoniously to the achievement of my choices or desires.

First and foremost, **I am me and I am my creation.**

The nature of any sentient creation, of any conscious creation, and of ALL creation, is to do all things about and for itself which could be considered beneficial and salubrious.

It is built-in to the nature of existence to support itself with wholesomeness and individual continuity.

Recognizing this all seek to do all that which is supportive of their life expression. Theoretically, all healthy organisms seek to promote and prolong their own existence.

Morality will not make a creation of mine be more normal seeking the continuity of his life and welfare when that creation does not function from its highest and best—i.e., the organism is not healthy.

Our thinking about morality has validity only when considering an unhealthy organism. Something which is not functioning for its own highest and best, will thence not be functioning for the highest and best of all of its creation.

Whenever I consider **me** I consider a healthy organism.

Whenever I consider **my creation** I consider a healthy organism.

Whenever I consider **an unhealthy organism** I am unhealthy and I treat my creation as unhealthy and therein the need for ethics is required so that a system of moral standards and values must be established. The innate capability and response is redefined according to a sick code of living. Whenever a society is seen which operated from a code of ethics, it is obvious that it is not acting in the best interest of itself and its creation.

Another definition is that **morality is right conduct** because it reflects the highest code of ethics for an expression. However, by saying this, power is given to the words as defined by humanity and are in that manner limited.

This is a game often played with morality being right conduct. It is from this point of view that most manipulate these words to be "their morality" and "their right conduct" as opposed to the morality and right conduct of another culture or civilization.

If, truly, what is meant that the innate "character" of a being is expressing itself to fulfill that which reveals itself and its absolute nature to its highest and best—this would be another story. For an archetypal pattern exists for the expression of all creation. This prototype does not insist upon what is to be "done" but rather is the vehicle through which anything is accomplished. The divine program for the vehicle to express is faultless. The selection of one step following another, one word following another, one thought following another, is relative to the individual use of their own programing. The prototype is perfect. How the individual consciousness chooses to use the vehicle is *the telling thing.*

Ultimate Calling

The ultimate calling of the spiritually directed consciousness is that of living fully and well from its inner awareness without any outside or otherness control.

When, and for convenience sake I will speak of humanity though I include at all times animal, mineral and vegetable in this concept, I recognize that the divine man lives in purity and perfection at all times, I am perfectly outpicturing all that is my highest and best.

The ultimate human is one who is guided by my inner rhythm and vibrates in the highest my harmonious chords can receive.

In me is no judgment.

It is judgment at all times which destroys.

For judgment determines what is going on in my thinking. I am saying that health is good and sickness is not good; I am saying that money is good and the lack of money is not good; I am saying that the successful achievement of what I determine to be worthy is good and the unsuccessful achievement of this is not good.

When the ultimate being sees all from the ultimate point of view it recognizes that all holds only one category, an IS.

As an IS, nothing has any judgment. All is an expression of whatever choices humanity has thought for itself. In its thinking it sometimes thinks that it would rather not experience something. This "would rather not" becomes a "would rather" and in this positive frame, brings about that which it says that it is not interested in having and knowing. This is the action of the Law of cause and effect, and so long as humanity recognizes the diversity of action of its expression rather than the onepointed attention to its choice, so it is.

I am a game player.

I love game playing.

Humanity loves games.

Humanity is a game player.

I am onepointed. Humanity, at times, creates itself as lacking in being onepointed. Whenever it does, it experiences duplicity. Humanity can know the purity and definiteness of its choices and actions once it develops within itself the consciousness of being single minded on any of its goals or choices. This does not seem to be too interesting to humanity and they would rather I create a moral universe—based on my judgment and rules—and force everything and everyone to fit into my morality.

Such force will never make reality different from that which it is. Reality will at all times move one IS at a time to another IS and never will the two be united, save in the illusory attitudes of humanity's thought system. No matter how real an illusion may be it will never be reality.

Morality is not the ultimate calling. Morality is too fractional. Morality is too dependent upon the vagaries of its capricious framers whose erratic conduct brings them confusion and incomplete results.

The ability to be master of all of the converging concepts which seeming righteously have control over my thinking as humanity is a condition I have allowed to take place in my mind. I was at one time totally free from such irrational attitudes for I was "born" into a vehicle which selected from the infinite storehouse of concepts those attitudes which I choose to experience. I am born in an environment, society and culture which inhibit or which delimit my thinking. I choose one culture or another at birth. In this choice I choose a given set of circumstances because I feel they will enhance and strengthen my outer responses. If I choose to be born into a given environment it is because I am interested in the challenge it gives to me. I can choose to be born into bodies less than perfect from one point of view, and into homes which are supportive or not, and a large variety of possibilities.

Also, I can choose to be born into a community which is fully harmonious. I can choose to create about me a theater or movie of nonviolent, nonintrusive and nonexciting experiences, but the very nature of humanity demands something which stimulates the adrenalin glands secretions which provide mankind with amazing strength and vitality under pressure or emotional trauma.

Pseudomoralism

Morality defines a moral quality of character, and living in accord with the principles or standards of right conduct. This is a pseudomoralism. People who choose moralism "affect" it and my pretending life is a sham which everyone can perceive.

I, of myself, as god, have no moralism. I do not define myself in relation to any other being or any other circumstance. I know all based on who and what I am and being all that I am, all is all. All is based on my own expression and experience.

In humanity the duplicity of moralism is seen everywhere. In this, it is natural that those who are just developing their moral conscience have few role models to follow—and certainly none with a deep inner conviction and integrity which does not falter at some later point in the game.

It would be easy to begin to list the malfeasant characters of society for they are everywhere and abundantly so.

More nobly sought are those who have the strength of their principles, character and integrity. Just as we are about to point to any of these, their *feet of clay* become exposed and in some way or another, and perhaps in many ways, they are found to be wanting in integrity by civilizations standards.

Perhaps my probing for the **perfect man** should not be tied to the rules of cultures, but rather to how well any individual practices the philosophy which he espouses; how well does the individual conduct himself in relation to the principles he holds dear; and how well does the individual stand as a living example of the divinity which dwells within everyone. These would be the telling criteria for any "perfect man" should he even exist.

My first thought goes to the spiritual masters of all time. Heading the list are Jesus the Christ, Buddha, Lao Tse, Confucius, great *Old Testament* masters, and leaders from every faith. But are these really examples of the perfect man? Each of these men faltered seriously as far as their community was concerned. Each was found to be less than noble in his society and his civilization. All were found wanting from the societal point of view.

Let's look at them from the true **perfect man** point of view. How well will they settle in here?

Jesus lived what he believed. He always stood up for his principles. He was a teacher and sharer and in this his methods of sharing could well have stood in the way of him being a living example. For he often had to use powerful illustrations with himself at the heart of the example to put across his point. He exhibited poverty, hunger, lack and no reputation the **perfect man** would outpicture—this is not what society would suggest. He was, in fact, so miserably misunderstood he was crucified.

Buddha violated rules his society taught and abandoned his home, his family, his responsibilities in his "family business" as a future king to be a vagrant vagabond. He was in contradiction to the local religion. He died eating tainted food. He had nothing and was taken care of by a follower. Undoubtedly there would be more should we search the records.

Lao Tse, Confucius, great *Old Testament* teachers, and others also led less than fulfilling lives. They knew social grace and much social disgrace. They knew poverty and wealth, back and forth. They had their ups and downs and were chagrined by their world numerous times for not fulfilling either what they said they would do or what their group expected of them.

It would seem that living from the divine within, following the principle and living according to the integrity of one's soul would certainly be a most harmonious life and living. Not so!

The great experience and the great fulfillment come not from a life filled with the luxury and soft living wealth are considered to bring, but rather in the inner sense of wellbeing which says *well done, my good and faithful servant.* It would seem that this were hardly enough for anyone who with sincerity and integrity lived the principles which were held dear.

When I arrive at a state of consciousness wherein I feel at peace with myself, when I feel that I have done "right" not by the code of conduct of any given society or civilization, but rather because I listened to the indwelling spirit which is always speaking strongly and powerfully to me telling me that which is beneficial for myself, that which though not beneficial, is the fulfillment of the principle upon which I base my life. These are the issues that are most important to all and give peace of mind beyond measure:

- The smile a mother has when she sees the wisdom and thoughtfulness she has trained into her daughter, being lovingly expressed without her directing her to do so.

- To any teacher when his student excels.

- To any sharer when that which he has shared is being lived by the ones with whom he has shared.

These are the rewards and treasures which are greater than all the gold, greater than all the wealth, greater than the fragile perfect health, harmony, right action, peace, and other virtues so desired of humanity.

The inner treasure is the reward which comes to the Jesuses, Buddhas, leaders of every dimension that all the morality and social righteousness falls far short of appreciating.

As a thespian may give the greatest performance of his life and inwardly know that this was his greatest expression as an actor—the applause of the audience goes unheard while the inward satisfaction and confidence remain alone to be known by the soul of this accomplished actor. Money and applause, acclaim and recognition by all are nothing compared to the inner awareness of confidence that remain perfect.

To a spiritual master one cannot give gifts for they are superfluous. To god none can give any gift, to creation none can give any gift. The only "gift," if gift is correct to name it, is the presentation of a life that lives fully and well the principle upon which all life is founded, the integrity of the consciousness to live what are the values most important to the ultimate of thought.

My life, as god, is a total giving to everyone everywhere, all my creation, so that whatever it is that any would like to be and know in their experiences, they may.

I, as god, make no condition on what the experiences may be. I give totally to all that they may enter into whatever it is that will fulfill their choices of whatever pleases them.

Morality is a game and a delight for all who enter into its experience. But always the game. For me it is the illusion of temporary action that is ever changing.

∞

9

ME EXPRESSING AS LIFE IN ANYTHING

I am everything, therefore whatever I create I express myself as that which I create. I am LIFE, hence all existence contains in it LIFE.

I am the life that indwells animate and inanimate substance, that indwells visible and invisible essence, that is surrounding all as its permeating beingness, without which nothing would exist.

It amuses me to consider how small my creation often think of itself. All the illusionary world contains the presence of LIFE in, through, and about itself—everpresent.

The life which is the animating intelligence through and around every concept, idea, illusion or reality is concurrent with that which exists.

Some would say it is separate from that which exists, but should it ever be separate from that which exists, that which exists would not exist. It would not exist either as a thought or as an ideal in the infinite storehouse of all.

Life is not something which is infused into something and which is then removed from something when it ceases to be utilized. Life is always present in an atrophied illusion or in a vibrant expression or appearance.

The appearance that life leaves a body when it is "dead" is only in the conception of what is meant by "leaving the body" as in death.

It is not difficult to conceive the life being present in the sperm and the egg, and this life becomes more vitalized as the sperm and egg join to enter into a new phase of creation. It is not necessarily that the phase they are entering into is one which must take place as a normal response to the pattern of expression. Rather it is one of an infinite number of possibilities which might take place: An *to be or not to be* whatever condition.

The life is always there. The life is not infused in the conjoining of the egg and sperm, it is ever-present. The life does not change when the egg and sperm develop into a body which utilizes the life principle in yet another way. As the body grows and develops, ages and changes, reveals an infinite variety of possibilities, at no time does life come and go, it is always there. Life, in a fractional manner, could be considered as the air humanity breathes. Life could be further thought of as the water in which aquatic creatures express. Life could be considered as the thought atmosphere which permeates all consciousness and while never belonging to one, is available and in and through all, to be used by each as each chooses to use it. It does not become a more beneficial life or detrimental life, depending upon who gets it to use, rather it is always the same marvelous life, with the difference in its expression only in how it is being utilized by the one using it.

So a "dead" body uses life as a transition of the once physical expression to an expression of returning to dust and its ultimate atomic form—and thence to its nothingness. All the while life is ever in, through and surrounding all—whether it is, so called, being used or not, from an objective point of view.

Life In Animation

It is with no problem that humanity considers life in animation. Yet it does!

When humanity views machinery it instantly says that there is no life there. It is mechanical. It is without creative intelligence at work in that object, except as in its creation and the mechanism to keep it in motion, surely not a life force.

Why is it so difficult to conceive of life at work in all? Life does not say it must be expressed only in viably organic things. For to limit life to organismic functioning wherein an object having diverse organs and parts that work together as a whole to maintain life and its activities, also thought of anything resembling a living thing in its complexity of structure or actions, is to say that I, god, am not everywhere and in everything and working universally throughout all.

It is the consensus to say that life is expressed in animation, life is evident in movement, life is real only when it has a function and purpose for existence.

To say this means that the mental activity is not life in action. To say this empowers only physical evidence as expressing life in any realistic manner.

The thousands, billions, untold numberless thoughts that surge through the consciousness of every "living" essence gives truth to the reality that life is surely in the unseen, in the invisible. The tiny gray molecules of the brain are its thinking center and the white molecules of the brain are its channels through which the thought is directed to accomplish its purpose. The far vaster array of molecules are utilized in moving the electrical current of the thought to its end work. Within the tiny gray cells are the infinite workings of the life principle—but the life principle is also in the white molecules directing the efforts of the gray cells to their accomplishment.

Unseen by the viewer is the "thought" and "life" which surrounds every inanimate object as it is put through its paces. As the gear in a clock reacts to the effort of the spring that gives it a power to operate, turns the other gears which operate the further gears and ratchets, moving the hands of the clock in specific patterns to purposefully tell the time to one who has learned how to read that time—this is life intelligence at work permeating and controlling the clock to achieve its goal or purpose of being. Though this intelligence may not at "this moment" seemingly be working through an organic essence, it worked through such in the creation of the clock and its operation. However, because the apparent intelligence of the consciousness which designed and invented the clock appear not to be present as the clock continues its marvelous work—they are joyously eternally present. The intelligence which framed the clock and its program remain forever present, whether the clock is operating or at rest. The intelligence, the life, is everpresent.

This can be visualized in an airplane, a television or radio set, in a can opener, in a pencil or computer, regardless how mundane the vehicle, the life principle is always present expressing itself in the intelligence for which it was garnered. Though the thinker seems not to be present during the operation of the equipment or object, the life principle as the thinker is always at all times present.

Humanity has had many experiences during which it has felt that a presence was present though unseen. This unseen presence is not unique or unusual, it is very common. Whenever a life has an affinity to that which it creates or enjoys, its presence as a life substance is knowingly there. This does not mean its presence seeks to control or overwhelm the area or condition in which the awareness of its presence is, but rather it cannot help but be there, as the life principle cannot help being omnipresent.

These remarks are made not to empower the reality of all being universally present, but to point it out as a salient fact.

I am known, as god, to be omnipresent.

I am wherever I am and all that I am is wherever I am.

There is no "part" of me that exists anywhere in my creation. Wherever I am in my creation, I am totally there. I am infrangible. I am indivisible. I am unable to ever be less than all of me. Though my creation may seem to be using part of me, part of my allness, part of themselves, they actually have that allness in and through them and around them to utilize when and as they choose.

When a man is speaking he is not singing. When a man is writing he is not swimming the ocean. When one does anything to the exclusion of something else, it does not mean he does not have the capacity to do something else whenever and however he chooses. All the possibilities are present in him at any moment to do whatever he chooses, but only when he chooses. Should a man ever truly desire to change the race consciousness about himself wherein it says he is able to think only one thought and do only one thing at a time, that can take place, but by his choice.

The possibility of the mind of man is infinite.

The possibilities of the expression of life is infinite.

The potentialities of all are PRESENT awaiting utilization, and they can be done easily and perfectly whenever it is the choice to do it. It has been the choice of humanity to limit itself and say that its limitation is its creative limitation. This is not so. All creation has within it all that I am and all that I am it may do the instant it chooses to do this.

It is inherently lazy and for this reason it chooses not to be responsible for its vast potential.

This need not be this way. I am expressing as life in everything. I am eternally available to all as myself and as life, I am available to all of my creation as it may choose. If it chooses to take only a small portion of my infinite beingness within itself, then that is just what it has permission (from itself) to do. I do not need to be limited, my creation does not need to be limited, the allness and nothingness are not limited.

It is the time of opening the doorway to the essence of all that is good and beautiful according to human standards.

I Am The Reality

That which appears is not the reality.

The reality of anything is the unseen force behind it, that which is the pattern allowing the atoms to form into the mold that is seen as an appearance. Even while the form appears, the reality behind it is ever revising itself, adding to its concepts of how it may best be expressed, and opening itself to greater and greater fields of revelation—so that what appears is in constant change and only that which stands behind it, its reality, its allness, its concept, fully complete, never changes.

Since stability stands in the power behind an appearance, any illusion may be redesigned freely and easily whenever it is the choice of the creator. This means that humanity need not be limited by the things it sees in the world about it, but it may move into the unlimited realms of imagination upon which it touches from time to time, but not with any definiteness and purpose.

The scientists, the artists, the poets and writers are they who have learned to reach into the field of illusion, into the area of imagination, to the dreams and visions of what might be, what are, and what comes forth. They probe into this field of creativity and come forth with concepts and creations which are a blessing to all humanity.

They do not "find" these miracles and magical wonders because they believe they are not there—rather it is because they do have within them the spark of creativity that brings out all of the wisdom and uniqueness which heretofore had been unrealized.

They dream. They invest their life principle in these dreams. The dreams come forth enfolded in their life and power and to the extent that they stand by their imagination and let it fully evolve, it does open itself to full manifestation and realization.

Glass has always been the best source of mirrors and lenses used to look at the stars and see the infinity of the heavens. One scientist chose to take mercury, which is liquid at room temperature, and use it to create a mirror lens with which to read the story in the stars. It could only read straight up because of its liquid nature, but it did read this way perfectly well. It did not take years of polishing nor specialized cutting and careful handling, because the lens is maintained in its perfect parabolic shape to give its perfect vision. The liquid metal allows the concept of the life principle being present, but it is equally present whether it be in the liquid movement, or the invisible microscopic movement of the atoms within the substance, and the movement within the atoms themselves, all life vibrantly at work expressing movement and purpose and enjoyment.

Scientists looking microscopically to the skin of a human sees not only its infinite number of cells, but the vastly greater number of living creatures on the surface of the skin called mites. What appears to be one thing, is not one thing, but many things. When humanity limits itself to thinking that *what it sees is what it gets* is so far from the truth, from reality, as to be as the mite on the human skin, not seen, but there, and we do get all of those mites whose purpose and work, while not yet known, will surely prove to be something beneficial ultimately in the ongoing understanding of all.

Just as the unusual may not be known because it is not seen, so the dreamers, the creative souls of the universe, touch within themselves to find that reality which stands there awaiting to be realized.

It does not matter how strange or how bizarre the dream my be, trust in it. For humanity has not even begun to see the realm of the infinite and its potential. The infinite number of dreams that cross the threshold of humanity's thinking have not been cataloged and recorded for posterity. As the snow flake has its diversity and uniqueness without number, so the numberless dreams, the infinite visions, the stretch of the imagination lies awaiting the probing of humanity through its most capable mental action utilizing the brain to achieve the heights of miracles, magic and infinity.

I am reality.

I am the revelation of the infinite cosmic imagination of the divine through life.

All of the strange and wild imaginative creations that the mind of man can envision—is reality. Each as an illusion given solidity and apparent reality (or physical sensativeness) may be demonstrated in the life experience of anyone who chooses to play the game of "reality" with any of these illusions. It is interesting to see that these appearances ever changing are given more power and potential "reality" than that which is the reality of all—that which is unseen. The unseen hies back to principle and in its invisible form reverts to its original cause of being an IS. As it is this IS, it is without relativity, it is without comparison, it is without need or wants to fulfill itself, it truly is.

This is the reality of me expressing as life in anything.

This is the fact that I am each IS, I am each relative illusion as a relative illusion, I am each comparison comparing myself to myself and always being exactly the same, the illusion fades and the reality remains.

Me expressing as life in anything is my reality. Me expressing as life in everything is my reality. Me expressing as life is all that is. I am LIFE. ∞

10

WHY I DESIGN AS I DO

I do not design!

All already is.

All already is formed.

All is already a unique concept fulfilled in its creative idea.

Humanity has heard the thought that there is nothing new under the sun. It is told numerous times that every thought that ever could be thought has been thought and so every thought is an "old" thought and every idea is an idea that already has been carried out an infinite number of times by an infinite number of beings in an infinite number of civilizations, societies and cultures.

This being explicitly true, mankind might well ask, why should it go into the realm of expressing that which has already been done, wherein then is the delight and charm and newness! All is so barren of purpose and creative fulfillment.

It is true, all relative comparing and joining of each IS exists in its ultimate permutations.

Relative Comparing

All is relative comparing—and this is the key word here, relative! For in its relativeness reality gives intonations of itself, opening inner fields for the mind of man to harvest and enjoy. As man intones the opening concept of any dream idea, that which is the reality of the dream translates itself into that which can be understood by humanity and therein enjoyed by mankind.

This is like telling a story with its many abridgments. In this the story is condensed from its larger format by omitting the seemingly less important parts, keeping the main contents more or less unaltered. The synopsis, while enchanting and interesting, does not have the smell of the flowers, the colors of the blooms, the height of their stems, the setting in which they grow or the magic of their existence. True the abstract of the main contents are there but they only point to the music of the story. The digest gives only its epitome as a statement of the essence of the story in its shortest possible form.

Relative expression requires all of the perfect fragrance and color and dimension and attitude of the experience be full blown. The imagination comes into play here. It gives depth and color to the picture and makes out of it a motion picture full of action and interrelationships and interemotional responses to the story at hand. Now the relative epitome becomes a plastic masterpiece for the enjoyment of all those who will take the time to entertain the adventure.

As in modern computer technology software programs are devised which can take billions of bytes and condense them into half a billion bytes or even less, depending upon the type of creation being condensed. Programs full of flowers and fragrance condense more completely than programs filled with essential numbers and incompressible information.

This same concept is true of the infinite expressing as an IS. It is quite easy for humanity to be given a word or concept and told in the game mode to pretend that they must give an entire description from the statement or word describing the essence of a subject in the shortest possible form, or its epitome.

Given this contest, and given the word God, every being will describe it according to his own heritage of information. It will be described on the scale of the omni everything, on the lawgiver concept, as the principle, as the father personification, as the mother creator realization, and hundreds—nay thousands of other predescribed virtues (and vices) attributed to the concept God as understood by those participating in the game.

While some of the responses may be true in the bigger picture and may in fact reflect the reality of god, actually few will fall into this category since few have allowed themselves the permission to think as BIG as god actually is in the reality of all. This is why books are written on the theme: IS YOUR GOD TOO SMALL! Too many visualize god in their own countenance and in their own image.

Countenance Of god

I question here the countenance of god purely to search out what man's thinking is relative to what he believes god is and how god responds as the ultimate design of all.

The face and nature or feelings of god reveal my approval or disapproval, support or lack of support and sanction, my calm control and composure, the way god looks as man visualizes it viewing humanity and being tolerant of what mankind does and his purposes for doing anything.

Though I do not have the countenance visualized of me by my creation, this is how they respond to my beingness. Since this is how they respond to my beingness, this is the limitation they place upon themselves of their relationship with me, the absolute infinite god.

The expansiveness of humanity indicates the potentialities which may flood forth as experiences in their lives, should this be their choice. I am unlimited. I am the expansiveness of the allness and express this way in all I create and am because this is my nature. My nature may be seen in its microcosm or macrocosm—in its finiteness or in its infiniteness. The choice is solely up to the viewer. Also, the viewer may change from one point of view to the other and back again constantly and I will never be disturbed by this infidelity to purpose, I will be in my creation whatever it conceives me to be. It will be whatever humanity can accept of my allness. The more mankind trains itself to have a bigger view of god and a larger concept of itself as the creation of god, and being god itself, the more fun humanity will have in being me and being its concept of itself. The entire design and creation of humanity and how it accepts the patterns which I as man demonstrate in its environment are no more permanent than a snowflake on a warm leaf in the sun.

What is considered designing is me as my creation patterning all ideas into a unique—for the relative human who seeks to fulfill his imagination—expression!

I, as my creation, now enlarge my focus and create the great motion picture of life. I gather together all of the themes which I wish to express in the film called my life. I determine at the outset what will be the highlights and the supporting issues which guide and direct me along the pathway to the completion of the story of my life.

I choose to live in a temple of the living spirit, my body. I name my body good and very good. I daily attribute all the lovely potentials of whatever I can conceive a body to be beneficial to me and lay claim to its expression in me. Even while fledgling and unseen by those about me, I constantly affirm my reality and express it in my world because I have named it and claimed it as mine.

As I grow in purpose and wisdom I choose to prepare myself to live in a positive body and a positive world. I take control and appoint myself my selfleader. As selfleader I follow my own attitudes for myself and ignore all about me which might be to the contrary. I build a strong body and a strong personal conviction of my own worth. I like me immeasurably.

This proves to be a glorious experience because the evidence is seen on all sides and in every aspect of my being.

I make the most out of every experience I have—a natural born leader, a natural born confident individual, a natural born loving being who admires myself and everyone I create about me in my world. I live in a selfcreated harmonious world of infinite peace and goodwill.

In my education process I am a winner. I choose to delight in all my subjects, not because at the moment I understand how they fit into the big picture, but because it is my choice to be a well rounded person and a harmonious humanitarian. As I do this I find that I am a fine student. I find that I am a respected student and supported by my peers in my choice of studies and they enhance my learning experience by their thoughtful questions to which I am able to stand tall for their answers.

Confidently I live in my family, regardless how others may view my family, for me it is perfect. I live confidently in my educational environment and am respected and admired for my capable thrust into all of the learning therein gained.

All of this is my choice, knowingly contracted.

I might think from time to time that I am having a difficult time to get cooperation and support from those in my world—but I instantly realize at moments like that, the only support I can count upon is the support from the spirit indwelling me. This is the coming of the dove of awareness into my consciousness and wherein I am aware that *I am proud and honored in my creation* and so it is. The power to accomplish and to be come from within each of my creation. I am there at the center of all of my creation empowering each to be all they choose to be, indeed all they are capable of being. Their capacity is infinite, even as I am.

This becomes a wonderful program of choices and of dimensions of awareness. As I am aware of my allness, so each of my creation have the same quality of awareness should they choose to aim from the relative to ABSOLUTE, to the reality, to the god concept. The god concept is clear and pure, the god concept delimits how humanity conceives itself to be. The term of limitation is over for mankind as humanity turns in, instead of outward for their study of themselves.

The New Man

I, as humanity, appear to design new things while in the ultimate all already exists and imagination, dreams, intuition, inspiration, illumination and their theme purely reveal to the relative human thought what already exists and can exist for humanity if it chooses to conceive that ideation.

Having chosen to grow from a fledgling youth into a divine man, humanity may use the tools of dreaming to achieve every choice.

The training of the physical educational center, the body and brain, have provided a fit vehicle for spiritual evolution to reveal itself. This vehicle has total selflove, total selfconsciousness, total selfawareness and lives in this revelation. Now with this trained educational center ready to go to work, the development of the higher virtues, the more intensive channels of reception may be entered.

These channels are those of imagination, dreams, intuition, inspiration and illumination.

Training itself to tune into these fields of cosmic consciousness requires a freedom of the spirit and a refreshing attitude toward itself that is rare in the fulfillment of this miracle environment.

The design technique that I am searching out in my creation is the tool of imagination. With this the wellsprings of unimaginable vistas of thought come forth. The ability to listen within is something that is developed by humanity. Normally humanity tends to turn itself to the outer tangible universe which it calls its reality; however, the only reality is the invisible and conceptual imagination which opens the doorway to areas not demonstrated heretofore in this dimension and in this span or time period.

The imagination, the expression of any concept or idea, has been fully revealed and fulfilled dozens of times in the history of creative imagination. That this is true, there should be evidence of this from time to time, but in my creative spirit and purpose in making humanity think that their thought is the first thought of that imaginative concept ever thought, I hide the evidence of past revelations. However, to the investigative consciousness, each has the power to delve into the past in such ways that all is revealed to them of everpresent incarnations of various activities. Also, in my creative imagination I create those delving into this as ***not*** being scientists who feel they must report this to their peers. Some do get through, but the essential ones do not. For this is part of the enthusiasm and joy of living as human beings, the mystery of life, the unknown of what lies before each. Precognition seems like such a desirable thing, but it falls far short of the program by which general humanity has chosen to guide its life and affairs.

It can be an avenue of humanity through which it expresses, but for the moment, it seems that it is to be a channel few will utilize because it is something that demands credibility for something which it has not yet allowed itself to feel is its privilege to experience. It is the privilege of humanity to experience the normal limitations it places upon itself. It has the lament that "Murphy's Law" is its reality saying if there is a possibility for something to go wrong, it will go wrong. So long as this is the theme of its thinking, mankind will experience this as its reality.

As a man thinketh in his heart, so is he.

This is a well worn theme, taught by every school of philosophy and psychology throughout the ages, even before philosophy or psychology were known as schools.

The image of mankind is only as limited as is its misuse of the principle—it should be said no principle can be misused. It can be used in ways contrary to what is outwardly said one wants but is obviously an inward desire of the heart. It is the most important thing to experience and all go for it tooth and nail.

The new man, the man of humanity who takes possession of his very soul nature, he is the one who rises in his use of imagination, who does not discount his dreams, whose masterful use of intuition reveals to him the magical marvels unknown hitherto now, who lives in the hive of inspiration letting it be his total guide and source of wisdom and joy, and he who chooses oneness with the illumination which surges forth from the very center of his being and never stops urging itself upon existence.

All of humanity has this **new man** in it and may let this **new man** shine forth, but the choice demands conscious control of every thought and every attitude and every emotional response to the universe in which it exists. This comes only through preparing the vehicle either before birth, at birth, following birth, or **now** to achieve this glorious result.

The **new man** knows the source of its genius and power.

The **new man** realizes that he must be living his life powerfully while all those about him may be following a different drumbeat. The **new man** walks his own way, keeps his own counsel, maintains his own intunement to his dreams, his aspirations, his intuition, illumination and imagination. He is his own master.

Why I Design As I Do

This is the opportunity all of humanity may know for itself. This is the design I have offered to all of mankind to follow. A false humility and a laziness keep most from following this pathway. To follow this theme is not for the dilettante whose superficial interest dies at the first scent of difficulty or obstacle, the amateur or aesthete finds interest in the possibility that someone else has or can do something, but seldom in the fanciful fact that they too can do these things. They shy away from the need to prove themselves in any sincere manner.

The representatives of humanity who achieve their goals are those who maintain their interest within themselves alone with no regard for what others can or have done. This is what makes the difference between wouldbe master expressions of my godself and those who powerfully and confidently claim the reality which I am in them. Humanity who find this their goal and purpose aspiring to its fulfillment, are given spiritual support in ways they are unaware but it comes without a doubt.

The confidence that humanity has in its ultimate goals and purposes are indicated by their own stick-to-it-ive-ness which remains unwavering under all circumstances.

I design as I do, being god, because this is all one grand game. I have created humanity to play specific roles in the game of being me and expressing me. The game is not to belittle the end result of humanity, but to let mankind know that since there is no other purpose to living than to *be themselves and have fun* then all of the seriousness is removed from the experience of life.

As my creation consider every experience, every action and reaction as a joyfilled event, every great blessing or apparent curse which humanity experiences is not an end and all thing, but rather it is only a move on the chessboard of life. It is an action which though in itself appeared to be unfulfilling, in the next game and the next game, and games numberless after that, the game can be played in any manner desired and in the playing of these games, nothing is important save to be yourself and have fun.

This being yourself would seem to be detrimental to others. If you are yourself you will always do those things beneficial to yourself and you will always act in manners harmonious with YOUR CREATION, the world about you. You will do all this because it is your design in being, my universal design for humanity.

Humanity will have fun too, because having fun is what it is all about.

Fun as defined by some is a negative condition. Actually by fun is meant here, doing that which is joyfilled and rewarding to ourselves and others. That which is fun is a delightful experience and supportive of salubrious welfare for all concerned.

This design is readily acceptable to all of my creation. It is something which already exists.

Humanity may take diverse paths in my design and wind up going an "infinite distance" to arrive at the point of being themselves. It does not matter in the scheme of things whether humanity does this or not, the only thing that matters is that humanity is being itself and having a good time, having fun, doing it. ∞

11

PUREST EXPRESSION OF MYSELF

Whenever thought is given to purity, it is usually meant to be that which is of unmixed character, virgin and in its simplest form of representation.

This is a definition capable of referring to anything. It represents the classic reality of any concept, idea or ideal in its absolute and uncomplicated essence.

To understand anything in this reference requires that the object be defined finitely so that whatever its purity is can be ascertained without question.

I define myself as god, the quality of being the Infinite and many names are given to me by my creation seeking to placate me. Yet all decisions to appease, pacify or mollify me are in vain, for I am at all times that which I am.

It is the definition which my creation gives to me which causes me to appear to be less than pure. Why would any creation do this to its creator when its creator's only purpose in creating was to give its creation "the" expression of itself. But my creation, living in a finite comprehension of itself, seek to create me in its own image of finiteness. This will always be a picture far from the reality which I am.

To attain the purity which I am my definition must be in its most fundamental form. To understand the purity which I am it must be realized that I am the all and the nothing. I am all and in that allness I am that without attitude, without emotion, without judgment, condition or duality. This concept alone of my reality confuses my creation greatly since my creation appears to live in a universe defined by these very circumstances which are an anathema to the purity which is my nature.

The purest expression of myself is the most finite infinite definition of who I am.

To say of me, god, that I am any of the following, is to put a cast on my expression and cage the very essence of my being from any type of expression whatsoever.

To say I am even *god* limits me to whatever the definition and heritage is that is given to this term by any culture, civilization or religion.

More terms are: *God, Lord, Jehovah, Providence, Heaven, Supreme Being, Almighty, God Almighty, Almighty God, Omnipresence, Omnipotence, Omniscience, Infinite, Everlasting, Absolute, Absolute Being, All Mighty, Maker, Creator, First Cause, Author, Mind, Divine Mind, Spirit, Soul Principle, Principle, Life, Truth, Love, Logos, Word, and hundreds more.*

Each term sullies the purity of me insofar as it limits my reality by definition. Anything which places a limitation on my reality takes from the simple purity of my essence.

I Am Simple

The great philosopher and spiritual leader of ancient times, Zoroaster, was asked by the King of Persia—600 years before the Christian era began—to tell about his religious understanding and define his God.

Zoroaster was a man of the soil and taught his many students gathered about him in his hinterland agricultural setting about the principle of the universe using the most simple illustrations.

When the king asked Zoroaster to come and teach him, the great teacher said he was not able to leave his students. The king asked him to give him some wisdom to take with him back to his kingdom.

Zoroaster reached down and picked up one ordinary seed from the dirt at the roadside and handed it up to the great king astride his noble horse, surrounded by his austere generals and horsemen, and said: "Here, great king, is my teacher."

The king was incensed. Irately he flung the seed on the ground and told Zoroaster he was a fool if that seed was his teacher.

Years later, after the king had returned to his castle and lost many battles, only then did he call upon Zoroaster to again come and teach him. Zoroaster again did not choose to attend to the king, but he sent one of his erstwhile remarkable students to wait upon the king's learning. The student was able to share with the king the way of humility, nonpossession, generosity and love for all, and an inner spiritual discipline which caused the king to completely change his expectation and presentation to his nation. The kingdom of Persia prospered greatly thereafter and was known far and wide as the nation of wisdom, peace and prosperity.

The king could have had his lessons earlier, for he was drawn to the Persian philosopher, but his cold heart would not allow him to accept Zoroaster's teacher, the teacher of everyman, simplicity.

Though all may not find my purity and essence in a seed, I am in everything and all things, I am in nothing and free as the atmosphere ready to be accepted as illumination, intuition, imagination and the dream of any who will accept this pure simple expression of me.

The seed, however, is an excellent symbol of my reality.

Within the simple seed is every answer.

Within the simple thought is every fulfillment.

Within the illumination flooding everyman's consciousness I am there seeking my self expression.

The elegance of this expression of me as the simplest and most profound seem at odds with one another, but only the one who can see the simple may know the most profound.

The phrase is often thought and sometimes spoken that we must have the pure simple open heart of a child to know the inner secrets of the universe. In this openness we "trust" or in other words, we are simple, artless, naive and without guile. This ingenuous quality of children allows them to be free from any judgment since they do not have the comparative life experiences with which to judge. The children accept things on face value and do not look for hidden concepts which would defile what they see and hear. Children are always looking for peace, harmony, love, truth, honor, wisdom, sincerity, and all that are noble virtues from their life. Because they expect to find these things, these things are found by the heart of a child.

In the purity of the dream fancy of a child great truths are revealed. Out of the mouths of babes come the eternal truths of the universe, it is said, and wisely so!

The essence of purity and goodness dwell in all consciousness. The godhead is considered my presence. This presence dwells in all of my creation. This present reality is the foundation of me present in every expression and circumstance that ever was, is or could be. **I am what I think I am.**

It is so exciting when my creation comes to the awareness that every thought that crosses the threshold of their consciousness is me expressing myself in them, calling forth the privilege of demonstrating that which I am in their everyday activity—in all my purity and essence.

Ultimately there will be a demonstration within any thought system of the imaginative possibilities and probabilities which reveal themselves now. It is not a matter of hoping that these dreams will reveal themselves, or that the illuminations will take place in the mind of each of my creation—they are and they do.

The situation is that my creation have not trained themselves to be aware of these circumstances taking place in themselves.

Though this is purely on the physical, the illustration bears fruit because it is the level that the relative man expresses and the level that the human being lives in a physical environment.

These human expressions may fly, travel mentally, live in any normally intolerable environment comfortably, know anything which it chooses to know, have the power to express its choices whenever it chooses to do so, be everywhere present with the full consciousness of whatever the imagination would reveal to itself.

These examples of transcending known physical laws or rules are not meant to supplant the physical conditions, but rather to show that there is no limitation to the allness of the universe. *Whatever the mind of man can conceive and believe, the mind of man can achieve.* This statement does not tie itself to anything that would tell humanity that it must express in one way or another.

I, as the infinite, can create out of nothingness the allness. I, as the creative cause of all, can bring forth from the void the universes beyond universes, and I can return the essence to its formless self once more, without needing a reason or having a purpose.

Could anything be more simple than to have a choice and have that choice manifest regardless of what "changes" in the objective world had to take place to allow this to come about. This is the ultimate of purity and simplicity. This is the essence of a child's thinking wherein the child achieves purely because the child chooses to achieve.

All Is Purity

It is the thought that something in the world of creation in which humanity lives is not good; to think such a thought means that humanity has the idea that somethings are impure. How anything could be impure when I am purity is beyond imagination. When all is pure, nothing can be impure.

Impurity comes from a universe which includes in its definitions the concept of dualism. For this duality which humanity loves to create on every side for what purpose it is difficult to tell, but of all the illusions, duality is the most fragile illusion. Duality has no substance to it. The only substance of the universe is my own reality and I am good and very good.

Everything which I am is pure.
I am everything.
Everything is pure.

Going from this syllogism to its effective fulfillment is a step which every thinking being takes perfectly. There is no other response which could be known and expressed.

The concept is most perfect:

To the pure all is pure.

Every thought that humanity may think is a pure thought. Each thought represents me speaking through mankind and expressing my own unique reality. The reason this purity is sometimes clouded is that humanity hear the words and ideas from me and interpret these concepts based upon their background, their heritage of thought and experience. From this point of view, rather than the pure thought, a variegated picture of the original is acted upon and the pure *first thought* is never known by the mind. The thinking center has no way of experiencing the pure thought because of the screen of images which cloud over the concept. This takes place again and again for one and a number of thoughts, until every thought is clouded in the impurity of interpretation and **the truth is never known**.

The Humble Succeed

Just as the Persian king could not immediately take the seed from Zoroaster as a learning tool, only later after his kingdom tumbled into an abyss that seemed bottomless, he remembered having met the great teacher who inspired him to take the step of humility, so for this reason he returned to this master sharer to gain from him what had to be gained so that his kingdom could once again prosper. Only as the king returned to Zoroaster with hat in hand, humility in place, did he benefit from the wisdom that had always been his had he only accepted and used it.

I, as god, do not ask humility from my creation.

I, as god, recognize that as my creation is humble to the indwelling wisdom which each is, only then does this genius come forth as a useful power in their lives.

Purity is *not* known only by its opposite.

Purity more readily means following the first thought and living by the principles and guidelines each establishes for themselves. Even the misers and rogues of society are successful in their purpose for they abide by the rules of miserliness or of being a rascal and a scoundrel.

Contrary to the attitude of many, everything in the universe is positive. Everything done in everyway to every experience is a positive undertaking. All actions and reactions are all positive.

Just as there are only positive circumstances in the universe, so there are only pure responses.

That was positively not done, that was positively done.

That was a pure thought, that was an impure (pure) thought.

Everything that is done is done perfectly and fully and well. There is no such thing that anything is contrariwise. Every action results in a specific reaction. If a hammer is used to pound a nail, the nail under the hammer moves into the substance in which it is placed while the hammer is pounding upon it. All things are positive, pure, divine—and good by my naming them thus.

I could rhapsodize over the purest expression of myself and sing with the words and sounds of harmony and love, but these too are merely objective statements of a very subjective expression which all in everyway ends up as an illusion or abstraction.

Even so, the abstraction is a wonderful outpicturing of whatever is going on in the inner self of all of my creation. As a mirror reflects back what it is shown, so the inner self of humanity reflects back to itself whatever it has first shown out of itself to the mirror. The mirror can only reflect what is shown to it.

We Use Our Inner Studio

The world in which humanity lives is one huge mirror reflecting back to humanity what it is thinking, its actions, its expectations and dreams from within the motion picture studio of its consciousness had projected through the camera of the eyes onto the screen of life.

This inner motion picture studio in mankind knows only goodness, purity and a positive attitude toward all of its creation. So as the work done in this studio is that of creating ideas and thoughts reflective of the self which it is, that self being pure, all that are projected are pure and positive. To think otherwise, means that the viewer is looking through the cloudy lenses of his own eyes, his own consciousness, at whatever experiences he chooses to know in his world.

The purest expression of myself, being god, is manifest through the purest vehicle of myself, which is my creation. All of my creation shine forth whatever it is that their interpretation is of me.

It is imperative that I am consistent in my belief of myself. For should I for one moment *choose* to establish a different cause relative to myself than my pure and positive cause, I would have another cause put into motion—equally pure and positive—and my life would be reflective of that cause.

Because I am god, I am at all times doing exactly whatever my choice is for myself.

I live in purity.

I am the purest expression of myself. ∞

12

WHERE DO I GO FROM HERE

Where do I go from here—

I am all that you (my creation) want me to be.

From the plethora of Gods you have created to represent me it seems that you have been unable to settle on one symbol surrounded by its definition which universally applies to me. I am all you want me to be. I am the grand image of a universal consciousness which encompasses the infinity of existence and nonexistence. *But I am also your choice* of a vindictive and judgmental overlord determining whether you, my creation, are worthy of continuing to be or whether in my wrath over your indiscretions I must destroy the lot of you and begin again, hopefully to a better conclusion than you have brought forth for yourselves at this juncture of your unrighteous evolution.

Who and what I am I will always be regardless of opinions, theories and imaginings of my creation of that which I am.

I do not judge my creation for that would be judging myself. I do all which I do because it is the fulfillment of my being and it is a joy to do it, it is fun! This same criterion I provide for all of my creation, animal, mineral, vegetable—or what have you.

For my creation, humanity, to gain the most from that which I am it is necessary for them to expand their awareness and view of my reality.

What Do You Want Me To Be

I am the reflection to you of what you believe you are. As you become aware of this inner dream and this inner conviction of your reality, then and then alone, will you begin to fully reflect in the world about you, in your body and your spirit, the fullness of that which I am. It is in this inner searching that all that I am as you begins to merge from illumination to manifestation in your life and affairs as a human being.

In no way is my desire for humanity that it have anything less than all which I am. It is my joy for humanity to have fun and be itself even as it is for myself. However, in the thinking system of man sometimes the things that are considered fun and a reflection of who they are is quite limiting and debilitating.

I illumine humanity to think of the greatest and grandest and most capable essence possible and know that that begins to describe me and my reality—and that also describes the man so thinking.

Whatever humanity wants me to be, it is.

This is why it is so vital that humanity build up the awareness within themselves of who and what I am so that they will have the clear picture within themselves of who and what they are. This is how I tell my story to mankind of humanity and of myself.

I go nowhere. I am everywhere. I go in the hearts of my creation as the most lovely reflection of myself and this is why I keep probing the thinking system of humanity to find ME at the very heart of themselves.

INDEED: **I am your greatest aspiration.**

I am the fulfillment of every dream or desire humanity may have ever entertained for itself and in this realization I am fully unlimited in whatever it is that I am.

Humanity can play on several levels of consciousness. It can play that it is subject to the physical body in which it dwells, that body which is called the ***Temple of the Living Spirit***. However, humanity belittles that body and places limitations on it. It says that the physical body is subject to its environment, to the content which came with it at birth of genes-chromosomes-DNA and a plethora of conditions which subject the body to respond in given ways to given stimuli. If this is the belief of humanity then this is the circumstance under which mankind acts and responds to the world in which it finds itself. That world may be a mental, physical or spiritual, it may be a universe that is provided for by other planets or other star systems or other attitudes of expression. It truly does not matter what the outer, when the inner thinks that it is subject to the outer limitations or controlling factors, then it is sorely so limited. All the choice of the individual and of the race consciousness of the individual environment.

I Am Your Most Sacred Limitation

It might seem strange to say sacred limitation but that is just what humanity does and it is just how humanity considers just what it is thinking about itself. It says that the infinite, myself, thinks less of itself than anything else in the universe. It says that I **want** something from my creation. Smile—how could I ever want anything from anything since I am everything and I am all. I truly need nothing, neither worship or gift, sacrifice or proof of the adoration of my creation, I am infinitely fulfilled eternally.

However, and this is always the case: I am your most sacred limitation. I am whatever you choose to think about yourself and whatever you choose to think about me is what you are. If you choose to think that I am the essence of the universe, so you are. If you choose to think of me as a demanding vengeful creator whose finger is constantly on you pressuring you to think, do, and be something which I expect of you in my harmful manner, then so it is.

Mankind does not have to be limited. My creation may have any provision that it may choose to have, as far as it can create to enjoy. This is the joy and fulfillment of everything that is desirable to experience.

Is your most sacred limitation an attitude about the ecology of the world? Just what is your opinion, your thinking, about your relationship and adjustment to other humans on planet Earth, the symbiosis between peoples, geographical areas, cultural and social communities, and the interaction of one with the other are of utmost importance when recognizing the sacred limitation in which each binds one another.

First I suggest to my creation, what I do with myself, I create all experiences from my own point of view, I love myself so I love my creation. I love and enjoy all that I do and I love and enjoy all that my creation does—regardless what they are doing, no matter how some creation may disagree with what some are doing, I love everything that each does at all times: **AT ALL TIMES!**

Since I do not judge anything any of my creation does I do not stand in happy or unhappy relationships with them. They just are and just do whatever it is that they do.

I look at the world and its inhabitants and delight in the creative imaginative ways in which it expresses itself. It is not the first time that this has been done. An infinite number of times this has taken place not only on this planet but on planes and planets of existence beyond number.

Environmental Convolutions

I am your expectations about environment.

For me to have the universe go through its gyrations and explode, evolve, exist or just be an IS, all are being myself and having fun.

To humanity the devastation of the rain forests, the hole in the ozone layer, the pollution of the cities, lakes, rivers, oceans and atmosphere are unthinkable, yet the destruction of these areas continues without letup even by those who protest it is wrong. Why is this so? Why would an individual who protests a condition himself contribute to that selfsame condition misusing environment as he conceives it to be misused; there is no one answer, but the most paramount response would be that doing these acts by an individual pleases that individual and expresses himself and is fun.

Horrors, you protest!

Smile, this is how things go and how life goes on. It is all the more evident by this action by this individual than millions of words or pictures over the experience of destruction.

I am your expectations about your environment.

I love everything in an instant by instant continuum. I am not a judge of the relative relationship one with another and one circumstance with another, I am independent of that, although I am aware of its illusory existence. I am also aware of its impact upon the members of society who will hotly judge everything about it. This does not give it any more reality than it ever had, for as a child may gather together his blocks and puzzles and scatter them wildly and peacefully play with them hours on end, so diverse is his attention to what he is doing, and nary a parent or adult would look on in judgment save to say, the child is doing his thing and having fun. That is sufficient for any explanation and it is also acceptable to any listener. Why not on the grander scale?

I am the creator. As the creator I look at my creation and smile. As the creator—just as you being a parent—I look at the works of my creation and call them good and very good. This goodness is hardly a judgment, but an acceptance on full face value of all that appears and all that is. I have created my creation well.

Caring—Sharing Am I

The word caring so often means that there is a personal involvement. I use the word caring rather to mean an awareness of, close attention to and a liking for those involved. Personal involvement means more to be troubled or burdened over the actions and welfare of another. I feel no need to protect or have custody of my creation. My creation is free to express in the diverse ways possible and, in this manner, to be as (societal reference) outrageous as imaginable.

I care for my creation with a loving attention to whatever it is that they do. I sit by in delight and watch as they build to their benefit or destroy to their detriment with no judgment on my part for any of their actions. I just smile and enjoy.

I am the illumination, the inspiration, the imagination, the dreams, the uninhibited dance of joy with which my creation fly. I am as the glorious sunset painted on the western sky. I am there. I am illumination and inspiration available to all whenever any would choose to look where I am, within them. So in the sunset, I am not intrusive, none may look or all may look, it does not deplete the power of my sharing. If any or all look at the sunset each receives their unique flight of fancy from the view—or none at all.

I care and share myself with my creation as a refreshing drink of cool water on a very hot day. I am there available. I may drink fully or sparingly. I may be shared or taken alone. I may be appreciated or spilled uselessly. To me I give because it is my nature to give and not because I am received, and surely not because I am received with gratitude. I give because it is my nature to give. Actually I cannot receive because I am all. However in humanity the desire to give is as the desire is in me—but when humanity gives for a purpose, either because there is a need or because it brings praise, then that giving is not a gift but a threat and request for a promise or a reward. Neither will be forthcoming for there is no one to carryout that request. From the beginning I am all and all is me, all is my creation, and my creation is me. Hence I neither give nor receive because all exists everywhere with all my creation and me.

Confidence In Relationships

I am your confidence in every relationship.

Since I do not recognize relationships nor do I conceive confidence, how could I be your confidence in every relationship!

I am your confidence in every relationship because I am you. As you I am your small self and your grand self. I am your limited opinion of yourself as well as your magnificent attitude about yourself. In being this I am that with each instant of your existence. As the term **IS** defines the relationship—there is no continuum, there is only the moment whenever and as ever it takes place.

When an IS exists, one cannot have confidence in what will transpire in a relationship that does not exist.

Why, then, say I am your confidence in every relationship. Remember, I am in you your creation of me as you and you have created me as the limited expression of all which includes both a desire to be, which is confidence, and an interaction between beings, which is a relationship.

Neither has significance except in the mind of the creator. Here YOU are the creator and you alone determine your limitations and your aspirations.

Why, when you know that there is no time nor space, there is no otherness than the now, no other being than you and who you think that you are, then why do you allow yourself to play the game that there is otherness and that there are other times: because you find it fun and you find it reflects your belief about yourself at this moment. So then it is okay to do just that.

Your Imagination At Work

I am your imagination in all your work as a creator.

As you think a thought and then because of your background and because of the manner in which you play games, you want to think in ways that are unusual and unrealistic, I am that imagination in you.

Since the sky is the limit, supposedly this is to mean that there is indeed no limit, I soar with humanity into the realms of infinite expression and flights of unique and romantic dreaming to come up with thoughts that apparently had never been thought before, or that were never thought in the combination with which they are being thought right now—this is the imagination which I pour forth to humanity and allow mankind to brighten their minds with the seemingly impossible and ridiculous concepts—that when carried out are of the most marvelous invention.

My imagination is your imagination. My dreaming and playing are the dreaming and playing of humanity just for the fun of it. Obviously there is no purpose to inventing and achieving ideas into a workable format. For these fade away just as quickly as they come. These are as useless as a sunbeam on a sunny day, there are so many of them that one is lost in the myriad others. Useless, yes and no. Useless as to purpose. Useless not to enjoyment. This is another of the many ways that humanity has of being itself and having fun in everything which it does. This is the essence of imagination. As a creator my work is letting the fire of imagination illumine my mind to fulfill amazing experiences.

Cause And Effect, Surprise Prayer

I am your cause and effect of your answered prayer.

The concept of god and prayer are synonymous. All of humanity seem to have the thought of god and prayer in the same breath everytime either comes up. God is all, as considered by humanity. Prayer is how god gives its allness to humanity, *humanity thinks!*

Prayer, as taught by great philosophers, psychologists and religious leaders, is a claim and affirmation. *Ask and ye shall receive.* Claim your good and experience it now.

All exists.

- **Prayer is not going to create something new.**

- **Prayer is not going to make something happen.**
- **Prayer is not going to change anything in the world.**
- **Prayer will set in motion a cause and that cause will reveal as an effect that for which a prayer is established.**
- **Prayer is utilizing the Law of cause and effect.**
- **Prayer is the act of saying that all exists and you desire to experience it in your world right now.**

As I god create the awareness of anything which I choose to know as a manifestation—as an IS it already exists. All exists as an IS and may be enjoyed by any who call it forth without reservation.

Prayer is communication with god at the center of man's being. Through prayer humanity opens the catalogue of the universe to both view and choose out of the infinite cosmos whatsoever it desires.

At all times all exists in this unlimited volume containing every paradigm, every parameter, every possibility—*there is nothing new under the sun*—so humanity uses its imagination and materializes any IS for its present use.

The Law of cause and effect or prayer—surprise—each is the same in its result. No surprise at all, smile.

∞

13

HOME AT LAST

I am always the game player.

Since I am all I am always playing and being relative. In this I express as a combination of IS uniting to create the illusion of a script being carried out which text can be added to, deleted from, or varied in any way at anytime during its execution.

However, since I am all I am playing being absolute.

What does it mean to say *Home At Last* when I still talk about the relative and absolute, it would seem they should be mutually exclusive! Truly not! Consider I am all. To comprehend I am all and I am nothing all at the same moment boggles the imagination however it is true. Since to say: **I am all and nothing** does not equate to the relative consciousness for which this is being written, suffice it to say *All and Nothing exist at the same time.*

Variety Of Dimensions

I express myself in a vast variety of dimensions. Each dimension has its expression by drawing upon the infinite source of the absolute wherein each IS dwells. Each IS, so to speak, stands side by side with every other IS; however, totally unrelated.

Each IS could be compared to a computer manufacturer's assembly line. Every computer part is designed to perform its role in "a" whole unit. Needed are an infinite variety of smaller subassemblies, a hard disk and its subcomponents, a chip holding its millions of subsectors, and the central processing unit, the monitor and the keyboard with its mouse. A wonderfully complex series of software or programs make the computer function with pleasure. Naturally it must be plugged into a power supply to set all this creation in motion, to have it work at all.

As each component, simple or complex, is an IS standing unique and seemingly purposeless alone in the array of IS, when a nonrelated thinker utilizes an idea to bring forth a creation, these components are called into play. All done to express the variety of dimensions possible.

Some of the levels include: *human, animal, vegetable, mineral, substance, energy* and *nothingness.*

On Being Human

A prerequisite exists for all existence: **Being Myself, and Having Fun! I am true to myself and I have fun being me!** After this prerequisite is met existence can go forth and express.

Humanity has chosen to develop a complex moral code by which it inflicts its various will upon its various members. It thinks this is its greatest and most harmonious pattern wherein human intercourse can practically take place. Humanity feels if these rules were not exercised turmoil and confusion would exist for everyone.

However if humanity took my **golden key**: *be yourself and have fun* as its criterion all rules would cease to have value and all conflict between humans would dissolve in a most exquisite harmony.

Humanity can never give to another or take from another for *all have all* and need nothing from outside themselves.

I have not placed one order of existence above another. I do not say humanity is superior to any other *kingdom* including: animal, vegetable, mineral, substance, energy or nothingness. Just as I would not place one human with any other and say one excels the other; nor say one member of any *kingdom* is more treasured or blessed than another. All relative objectivity IS and is perfectly what it is!

Every human whose modus operandi is to be himself and have fun creates about himself a world of utter harmony and abundance, of joyous relationships and wholeness of mind, spirit and body. Truly to establish bliss in the relative requires the ultimate balance within. The balance is obvious. I have made it this way. I have made humanity feel good about itself when it likes itself and has fun in everything it does.

The happy human is the one who is at home in himself.

The happy human is the one who knows himself and lives by the divine set of rules to fulfill whatever goals he sets for himself without haste, panic or any sense of urgency—yes these words all say the same thing but each word here has a different emotional hue for the individual. Each word challenges the individual rather than illumines him in his very special work.

Seemingly the human being is master over all other creation: **or** so humanity has told itself in its own creation story. Is this true or does *each unique creative expression equally have the opportunity to be itself and have fun*—I know so!

No creative expression has control over another uniqueness.

Humanity asks itself: If each expression defines its own expression and calls it forth, why do some experiences appear less than desirable—certainly not fun!

This too is a choice.

A positive thinking humanity cannot conceive of itself thinking negatively about its own benefits and yet it does just that far more often than it thinks positively for itself.

To illustrate this with a few examples, humanity rather says: *I can't; I don't know how; I don't know; I have much to learn; I don't like that food, job, person, place, thing;* and *finally they are smarter than I am.*

With ANY of these thoughts or thoughts like these humanity has claimed less than its possible choice. Humanity has the freedom to do either without recriminations, usually with sympathy.

Since I am god and I am good and I am all, then how could anything "not good" express in my world? Here is a powerful point I make—all is good, even the seemingly "not good" is good because all exists without judgment. If all exists without judgment, why do I use the term good—I use the term good while every choice humanity makes (I make) is a decision uniquely done purposefully. Hence good could define "beneficial choice" and not good could define "not beneficial choice" and everything is done by a choice regardless how subtle or unconscious, the seed of each choice was planted and how naturally it flowers.

Animal Dimension

I see all animals being themselves and having fun.

In my allness I am all, I am animal expressing the nature of myself born in my selected way as whatsoever animal I choose to be, doing all it is my nature to do harmoniously, easily and successfully. As animal, I have no fear of death because I do not choose to be aware of death. Should my instinct be mating for life or a motherly instinct for my young, these are just that, and I go my way.

I am in each animal whichsoever and that animal enacts whatever feelings, instincts or attitudes I create in it of myself. I create each one for my own purpose. As I eat my thoughts and words, so I create plants and some animals as my sustenance. I create some for a charm, for loving, for beauty or a hundred other possibilities. Each animal in my world is perfectly designed and wonderfully expressing. I create each good and very good. Even to bacteria.

Vegetable Dimension

As god I have a pleasure to create objects and substance to be as paints on a canvas to portray pictures of the illusory images in my mind. Naturally this is the relative mind. While the animal kingdom gave me creative variety, plants or vegetative or vegetable matter fall into an entirely different genre. I delight in creating life within objects which need no soil to grow but subsist from substances in the air, to vegetation growing as fungi having no chlorophyll as yeasts—molds—mildew and mushrooms, to plants drinking in sunlight such as great trees—grains—grasses and undersea plants. Scientists today count species in the millions and subspecies in the billions.

Such variety—each a pure delight to me. Each has the life I give to it.

No dimension more important than another and truly no dimension important at all should I choose to erase any one or all from expression. Each existence—each illusion—persists so long as it gives me pleasure to have it endure. When gone, it is no loss; when present, it has no purpose. Sometimes, however, I say it has environmental impact, so here as in reality the existence of my thought creation do not depend upon one another for their individual purpose. These are games I play for fun.

Mineral Dimension

To define a dimension "mineral" would seem to preclude its having "life" in it.

Every idea or concept has life in it. All I create has life in it. Each creation is created to carry forth the program I have for it. Should I delight in having the rocks and hills sing, so they would. Should it pleasure me to allow the blowing sand or the singing star to whisper vocally a symphonic orchestration across the dunes or across the light years of timeless time, each is heard by ears which know they are godears and which delight in hearing the mineral universe respond to its godnature.

It is limited for humans not to see me and their life expressing in clay, stone, water, minerals of every type—for the life and voice dwell therein.

Man loves precious stones and minerals and would die to possess them, man would commit any act necessary to control and manipulate these substances—and still man claims to believe no life dwells in minerals. This seemingly lifeless substance is sought after hotly.

Substance Dimension

The dimension of illusion is the dimension of substance or matter. Yet humanity knows full well the transient nature of any substance. The objectivity constantly finds the quarks (subatoms) which constitute any substance in constant change.

Were substance real it would be unchanging. Since it is always changing—as it is my choice to create it as an illusion—I utilize it in its changeable nature. All I create, every dimension, I create to express my imagination, my concepts, my dreams for it. In fact, I dream and then I create a dimension in which my dream may fulfill itself objectively and subjectively for myself.

I as god know no limitation. As god I need no reason nor must follow any logic to mentally and physically walk with that which I create. All I do I do to express my unlimited self and to have fun. Substance exists as a concept for me to fill in the molds of my imagination.

Energy Dimension

I create a power which activates my illusions. As my illusions are invisible, so the power which energizes the illusions is unseen. The joy of being the intelligence behind the thought which burst forth 20 billion years ago and out of nothing, itself the mold, allowed the universal energy to enfold the concepts to bring forth a universe so vast and unending in its expansion that it spreads forth as a drop of ink in a glass of water. The power of the energy is as vital in one area as in another—never decreasing in value regardless how widely spread or to the degree used one place or another.

This happens because I am the power. As the power I am infinite. I can never be more or less power for wherever I am I am ALL POWER! This power I am activates all life-ness on all dimensions of existence.

Nothingness Dimension

Humanity smiles as I refer to myself as the nothing and the all. Each is equal, each is the other.

The nothing is my sleeping imagination. The nothing is the energy of my allness expressing in potential its actual.

As a sleek healthy cat lies in apparent sleep, apparently unaware of the universe about it—

dwelling in the illusion of nothingness—until something captures its attention for the spark of lightening in the heavens has no force so immanent as the active alertness of an interested feline.

The illusion of nothingness leaves this potent energy dormant but not void of its power. In the instant needed the vital force bursts forth from its invisibleness to carry out its direction.

Nothingness is the sleeping giant while active energy is the awakened giant capable of unimaginable expression. Imagined by our dreams, our visions, our desires—nothingness releases all we can envision to take on an outer appearance—albeit temporarily.

My Reality

My reality takes on several expressions. I assume out of the infinite *an archetypal form* which is undefined and eternally the same; this archetypal form advances through the *concept or idea* which clothes the archetypal form with the substance of quarks; while nothing is either created or destroyed, all exist universally as an IS which retains its uniqueness but has no relativeness: until all dwells in anonymity as the absolute.

I am able to be infinite because I am infinite. The capacity of a human being to know and express divine qualities is in exact proportion as the development of man's brain to perceive. Occasionally a human is born a superior genius expressing in one area of his total genius. The person may be a whiz in mathematics, physics, music, art or—in a physical capacity—without any special training. Some train themselves to these areas and develop a talent therein excelling beyond measure.

What is taking place with inborn or developed genius is the natural or programed uncovering of the **oneness link**. This link in computer parlance is networking or linking with a "source" in which is the information or software necessary to accomplish amazing talents. Within every human being—et al—dwells this *oneness* sans link awaiting implementation. To implement the resident genius requires a training which goes contrary to everything humans teach to themselves and their young. A young bird is kicked out of the nest not because the parent wants to dispose of the young or kill them, rather because instinct says this is the next step of development in surviving, flying, living. Humans have surrounded themselves with so many appurtenances to do what once their brain and body had done so instinctual development stops, growth from the inner ceases and more and more accessories are added and needed to live comfortably.

- ❑ Man could think "warm" and his body would be in comfort.
- ❑ Man could think "being there" and he would be where his thought dwelt.
- ❑ Man could think "house" and it would manifest before him.
- ❑ Man could think "solution" and any solution needed would be there.

- Man could think "himself" howsoever and so it would be instantly.

However the choice yet remains open to humanity. Smile!

Archetypal Form

Before I manifest myself as a human being I flow out of my archetypal form. I, as god, demonstrate myself in infinite variety. I am man, woman, child, animal, vegetable, mineral, substance, energy and nothing. In this diversity again I choose a uniqueness, i.e. one!

However, in that *one* I choose a specific one among many. I also choose in the diversity of the one peculiarities which please me. Hence, I choose race, color, religion, birthplace, parents, community, environment, chronological period, societal position, and here too the list is endless.

Presuming I choose planet Earth my humanness would be fairly consistent unless I choose a mutated body or mind or life, or all three. Had I chosen another galaxy, another star system, another star for a sun, another planet, I might be amazingly different from an Earth creature.

Because I am god I make any decision based on what to me would *be me* and *be fun for me!* Anything other than that is unthinkable.

An archetypal form cannot come forth unless a thought decided upon that form.

Concept Or Idea

A concept or idea offers a direction in the imaginative creative process resulting in the archetypal form.

Out of the *one mind* which I am is thought any thought. I, god, do not think per se. My nature, of, in and by myself, does not include thinking. In my godnature or godself all IS. Nothing new is thought or perceived, all IS, was and always will be; because of this I cannot think, create or become anything which I am. To uniquely be any of the IS I am would make me that IS and not the I AM or ALL!

In the diversity and acculturation of the ISes there is no possibility I can be one and all at the same time; I can be all and include the one, but I cannot be one and include the all.

Only as a conceptualization or ideation can I perceive such an allness including the oneness existence. Insofar as it can be conceived it can be realized.

This is the most difficult level for my creation to accept. I am and I know therefore it is done for me. My creation are but as yet have not claimed that they know, so until each accept the possibility and ascend to the awareness, all lies beyond their experience. However, all is their experience the moment acceptance is made of the condition and all it entails.

I claim this awareness now.

Undifferentiated IS

In all things we choose to specialize objectivity to be contained within boundaries. These perimeters are selfinflicted, selfinduced and specious. Human life and thinking depends on viewing life and its experiences as apparently attractive, true, or correct but not actually so: deceptive. Humanity believes all is differentiated—a unique expression, a particular IS, while each IS is undifferentiated, totally separate from all other ISes, yet one as the whole.

So long as humanity chooses to differentiate itself naming its beingness and activities are special and individual, it cannot view itself in the field of reality in which it really exists—allness.

As me humanity can experience the illusion of unity in diversity.

I, as god, know I am all.

I, as god, know I am each IS.

I, as god, know I am all and nothing.

However, I, as god, do not visualize "myself" as being each separate IS. Should I so view myself I would exist in that limitation. Humanity, as god, can maintain this objective awareness and maintain its spiritual allness. It does take a disciplined point of view from which it dare not ever waver. For to waver all limitation incumbent thereto would have full power to manipulate and control my infinite world.

I, as god, exist only as the undifferentiated IS.

My Home As god

As humans who are vast in their awareness and their travels say of themselves, *home is where I hang my hat or home is where my heart dwells.*

My home, as god, is in and as all and nothing.

My world, my universe, my dwelling place transcends any description since my human pen may write of what it knows and use defined words to describe all its avenues of expression. The ultimate of god transcends Earth man's experience or awareness. Thus such a description reveals a minute portion of a vast world, galaxy, universe. Reasonably and logically a human must admit its limitation. I, as god, know no such limitation. I am over all. Yet this allness dwells solely in consciousness as thoughts or ISes. As I believe I must describe all from the relative viewpoint I see but a *pinprick* of the eternal.

Knowingness—The Relative

This is a lovely place to begin man's understanding of the infinite each is.

I know the illusory reality of the temporal world. In this I care. I know nothing in the temporal world can change or destroy my essence. I know the game I play in my home or homes—all, one, nothing. As such I see each adventure for what it is, an adventure, and I enter into its amusement, its pain, its satisfaction, its failure, all defined and created to be exactly for that purpose. For that game. For that accessory in my home.

My predominant attention resides in the human genre, everyday life with its dreams, wants, desires, programs and noble or ignoble gestures. Each gives me wondrous joy and fulfillment for this is the home I call my own at this dimension of my expression here and now. However there is a greater way.

ISness—ABSOLUTE (Unknowingness)

As a human effete, I choose to leave the effectiveless path, there is a way seemingly indescribable.

It is not done by lifting my eyes unto the hills from whence comes my help but rather from looking inward to the center of my being and redefining my reality in light of myself as an existent IS to myself as the I am, ABSOLUTE, the all. In this pattern I leave the plethora of relative expressions and as all exist in unknowingness.

My home, as god, is where I hang my hat, i.e. wherever my thought may dwell and express. But in the broader sense my home is in the allness.

I have taken a circuitous journey in this volume to finally return home at last.

I have wandered over the probable and improbable playing but a few of the many games I enjoy participating in being always myself.

Now I allow the probity of the ISness as divine to take its nonrelative station, now lacking integrity or human moral uprightness, to be eclipsed by its universal quality as ABSOLUTE.

The journey *Home At Last* need not be so traumatic. To pave the way I can keep on track with affirmations of oneness, of connected awareness of my infinite nature and my constant intuition as god, which I am.

I am that I am, I am god, I am ABSOLUTE.

∞

GLOSSARY

Specialized Terms With Their Meanings

WORDS HAVE MANY MEANINGS. Dictionaries give the most common usage of included words. In the Autobiography of god, *and other publications of God Unlimited/University of Healing and the University of Philosophy, expanded meaning—glosses, interpretations and usages—flow in and from words used in special contexts. The following list proves helpful to the dedicated student. Words easily found in the dictionary are generally not included here.*

Words and senses are born at a great rate.

It is the practice in UNI-published-books to run-on all normally associated "self" words such as selfrespect, selfdiscipline, but not unrelated words such as "self words." Such use in English is frequent and widespread according to the dictionary's section: EXPLANATION, NOTES, ENTRIES, MAIN ENTRIES.

≈ *this mathematical symbol is defined as: is approximately equal to. This reference helps define our use of words here.*

- **ABSOLUTE** ≈ positive, unquestionable, all (includes all creation–nothingness and allness, is the intelligence of the universe, is the cause and effect of existence and nonexistence, is the thought and unthought, is all purposeless existence)—for the fun of it

- **allness** ≈ the quality of wholeness, expression or condition of existence

- **anthropomorphic** ≈ ascribing human characteristics to nonhuman things, i.e.: thinking god has human responses and human reactions to human creation

- **archetypal** ≈ an IS, for which there is no other IS, the original concept, a perfect example of the thing itself

- **autobiography** ≈ the *self* story written by the one written about; with biography: an account of the life of something—anything

- **being** ≈ quality/state of existence, conscious existence, the totality of existing things

- **bliss** ≈ state of a master, untouched by life, complete happiness, paradise, heaven

- **Buddhist** ≈ one who lives their life founded on the teachings of Gautama Buddha of India

- **care** ≈ care is not love. Care is a belief that a creator should manipulate his creation (see Chapter 12, subhead "Caring—Sharing Am I")

- **carton** ≈ a container to enclose objects or ideas, all the ISes exist uniquely as one in the ABSOLUTE

- **cause** ≈ a choice made, a desire, a thought empowered

- **chance** ≈ luck, contingency and opportunity seem present but only one Law (Law of cause and effect,) governs all activities; hence, a cause was instituted on behalf of the "winner" which had not been done for the "loser," all actions are predictable to one responsible for his choices

- **chaos** ≈ the confused unorganized state of primordial matter before the creation of distinct forms, formless

- **child** ≈ innocence, clear conscience, pure, know no wrong, amoral

- **choice** ≈ suggests the opportunity or privilege of choosing freely, when done onepointedly the thing chosen manifests

- **Christian** ≈ one who lives their life founded on the New Testament, not necessarily a pure belief in Jesus Christ

- **creation** ≈ manifest thought

- **custom** ≈ applies to a practice or usage so steadily associated with an individual or group as to have almost the force of an unwritten rule

- **deity** ≈ the essential nature of god; divinity; god, supreme being

- **destiny** ≈ a wise counselor understands that if the present course of action and direction are followed specific result—destiny— will follow; should the course be changed the former destiny is invalid, but whatever choices are made a new "destiny" becomes an irresistible power or force to expedite the new end

- **divine** ≈ discovered intuitively

- **dualism** ≈ the concept that there is more than one power and intelligence

- **effect** ≈ the response of prayer, of an affirmation, of any claim upon the Law

- **enlightenment** ≈ is sought by those walking the spiritual/divine path, each reaching awareness of illumination calls it a final blessed state marked by the absence of desire and suffering
- **essence** ≈ ultimate nature of itself
- **fate** ≈ implies an inevitable and usually an adverse outcome based on a lifestyle, causes and actions all of which can be changed at any time to experience a "new fate"
- **first thought** ≈ the inspiration of our god nature; training to recognize it is man's finest duty
- **form** ≈ the shape and structure of something as distinguished from its materialism, the essential nature of anything as distinguished from its matter, archetypal concept-image-idea behind all that is manifest and not manifest
- **fun** ≈ the divine purpose for existence is *to be and have fun being*, a human condition, to be sure, fun gives: pleasure, enjoyment, well-being, contentment, ease, satisfaction, takes from none, does only fun for anyone else involved, implies laughter and gaiety; but, may imply merely a lack of any serious or ulterior purpose
- **gloss** ≈ explain, define, interpret, describe obscure words and expressions used in a special way, i.e.: *glossary*
- **God** ≈ *that* worshiped by an individual or a group, i.e.: Chris-

tian, Islam, Hindu, etc.

- **god** ≈ the undefined, undescribed, ultimate reality, principle, mind, ALL, nothing, creator, its creation, IS, a cynosure, ABSOLUTE

- **guru** ≈ an acknowledged leader, remarkable teacher and spiritual guide in Hinduism

- **habit** ≈ implies doing anything unconsciously and often compulsively

- **heal** ≈ to restore to the original purity and integrity

- **Hindu** ≈ one who lives their lives founded on dharma, dominant religion of India

- **honor** ≈ doing what it is one's nature to do

- **human** ≈ god is in all, as all, totally, but expressing as unique illusions such as: animal, mineral, vegetable, undifferentiated matter and nothingness. A human form is one of the many archetypal expressions of its "imagination"

- **humble** ≈ the act of recognition of the one power and intelligence god and knowing all this dwells within

- **humility** ≈ to fulfill all promises and pledges made, being a person of your word

- **illusion** ≈ perception of something objectively existing in such a way as to cause misrepresentation of its actual nature, visually, intellectually, psychologically, physically. All form is an illusion since each is in a constant state of change. All illusion is an objectivity of the essential form

- **infrangible** ≈ god, spirit, principle, one-pointedness, archetypal, first thought: not capable of being broken or separated into parts, impossible to be infringed on or violated
- **intractable** ≈ not easily manipulated, obstinate, unruly
- **intransigent** ≈ uncompromising, irreconcilable, refusing to abandon an extreme position or attitude
- **IS** ≈ an IS is the fractional segment of time that any object or thought or concept is expressing in a given wholeness; complete in itself without needing anything added to it or taken from it to understand its completeness (see Chapter 7, subhead "Concept Of The Is")
- **Islam** ≈ one who lives their life founded upon a belief in ALLAH as the sole deity and in the Prophet Mohammed
- **Jew** ≈ (Judaism) one who lives their life founded upon one transcendent God revealed to Abraham, Moses and other Hebrew prophets
- **Law** ≈ there is one Law in the universe, all other propositions are rules. The Law is the Law of cause and effect, for every cause put into motion an effect in the nature of the cause follows
- **life** ≈ life exists in all thought, nothingness and allness at all times, life is the intelligent animating principle
- **limitation** ≈ to think the infinite needs something of the finite in any way
- **logic** ≈ applied knowledge based on

relationships of ideas and concepts

- **love** ≈ the capacity to create and allow that creation to be that for which and in which it was created, total recognition that what any creation does is how its creator created it

- **man** ≈ humanity

- **matter** ≈ matter and energy are equivalents where energy equals mass times the square of the velocity of light, nothing becomes undifferentiated matter (atoms)—thought thought

- **matter** ≈ the substance of which physical objects are composed, transient, ever-changing, material substance that occupies space, has mass, and is composed predominantly of atoms constituting the observable universe, interconvertible with energy, the indeterminate subject of reality

- **monotheistic** ≈ doctrine or belief there is one god (mono/one, theism/belief in a God: Monad/one, atom)

- **morality** ≈ morals are the interpersonal civil manners and customs of a given civilization

- **-ness** ≈ a state or condition, the quality and degree of being; peculiar and essential character/nature

- **nirvana** ≈ final Buddhistic beautitude through extinction of desire and personal consciousness, bliss, heaven

- **nonjudgmentally** ≈ condition of observation without comparison [**-ly** ≈ manner or nature or appearance]

- **nonpossessiveness** ≈ the ability to experience, utilize and share talents and things, without any desire to claim them or repeat the use

- **nothingness** ≈ nonexistence, not manifest, no illusion, existentialless—having no being in time and space

- **omni** ≈ all; universally; god

- **omnipotent** ≈ a relative universe needs power to exist as an illusion. ABSOLUTE IS and as such powerlessness

- **omnipresent** ≈ just as the nothingness and the allness are one and are everywhere present, so god is universally totally present everywhere in the relative; in the ABSOLUTE there is no time or place and all is one

- **omniscient** ≈ knowledge is relative, naturally as awareness of the relative the essence of god is all intelligence, but should any item of knowledge be in god awareness god would be limited, god cannot be limited, god is allknowing but not unique knowingness

- **onepointedness** ≈ **one**/a single purpose; **pointed**/specific aim; **-ness**/quality, thing, essential nature

- **outpictured** ≈ physically or materially manifest or demonstrated [She outpictured a happy face] [We outpicture our inner beliefs by our physical body and our affairs]

- **part** ≈ there is no *part* of god that exists anywhere in god's creation, all of god exists wherever god exists and god exists everywhere

- **peace** ≈ oneness with and as one's godself
- **philosophy** ≈ *the love of wisdom*, the pursuit of wisdom, one's way of life based on his values and priorities
- **practice** ≈ suggests an act or method followed with regularity and usually through choice
- **prayer** ≈ the affirmation and claim we experience through every cause we activate
- **principle** ≈ a primary source: ORIGIN, original cause of the existence of an IS
- **reality** ≈ illusion is the mirror that reflects reality, the one archetypal concept, which upon the purity of the mirror, depends the vision of reality. The more perfect the mirror the more realistic is the illusion of its ABSOLUTE form as the ultimate IS
- **reason** ≈ information which explains conclusions in thinking
- **relative** ≈ not *absolute* or independent, a thing having a relation to or connection with or necessary dependence on another thing, the *illusory* based on or producing an illusion which is deceptive and only apparent because it is constantly changing, a human game of choice
- **religion** ≈ the evidence of one's philosophy of life, be it a standard religion or material achievements, religion is one's daily habit being the prevailing disposition or character of one's thought and feeling: mental makeup. To some it is their ADDICTION,

PRACTICE, USAGE, CUSTOM and WANT: means a way of acting fixed through repetition

- **sage** ≈ one wise through reflection and experience, profound philosopher

- **spirit** ≈ god, life, principle, universal presence of the infinite

- **spiritual** ≈ the movement of thought in the divine

- **thing** ≈ indefinite name for a definite object or circumstance; the concrete entity as distinguished from its appearances; *thingness* the quality or state of objective existence or reality

- **think** ≈ to form or have an idea or thought in mind; implies the entrance of an idea into one's mind with or without deliberate consideration or reflection and to onepointedly access the idea or thought clear of all rationalization or intellectualizations

- **thinker** ≈ one who thinks or is a receptor of universal unsullied thought ready to be acted upon; (see Chapter 13, Subhead "Concept of Idea") god does not think; out of the *one mind*, which I am is thought any thought; I, god, do not think per se. My nature, of, in and by myself, does not include thinking. In my godnature or godself all IS. Nothing new is thought or perceived, all IS, was and always will be; because of this I cannot think, create or become anything which I am. To uniquely be any of the IS I am would make me that IS and not the I AM OR ALL!

- **thought** ≈ the pure idea, a concept awaiting commitment; rethought thought and likely to suggest the result of reflecting, reasoning, or meditating rather than of imaging; claim your first thought and write it down instantly, then the ideal manifests; thought suggests to think is a process

- **trust** ≈ doubt that what should be the outcome of a condition will be its outcome hence the circumstances are manipulated calling it trust—expectation to do right according to the observer's anticipation and opinion

- **TRUTH** ≈ symbolically universal TRUTH is that which is unchanged and unchangable, always referring to essence, in universal TRUTH relationships do not exist

- **truth** ≈ in fact; in truth; in truth: in accordance with fact; ACTUALLY, truth is the objective appearance

- **unconditional (less) (ly)** ≈ participating in a relationship or an event without prerequisite, without covenant, without stipulation, without judgment; also, without even consideration of anything which normally would invite observation, however seemingly important

- **undifferentiated** ≈ essence with no defined purpose, i.e.: chaos (see chaos)

- **usage** ≈ suggests a customary action so generally followed that it has become a social norm

- **viable** ≈ substance capable of being motivated by life, an idea so capable

- **wont** ≈ usually applies to an habitual

manner, method or practice of an individual or group

- **wisdom** ≈ the ability to discern inner qualities and relationships
- **woman** ≈ humanity